Negotiation Booster

Negotiation Booster

The Ultimate Self-Empowerment Guide to High-Impact Negotiations

Prof. Dr. Kasia Jagodzinska

BEP

BUSINESS EXPERT PRESS

Leader in applied, concise business books

Negotiation Booster: The Ultimate Self-Empowerment Guide to High-Impact Negotiations

Copyright © Business Expert Press, LLC, 2021.

Cover design by Kasia Jagodzinska

Interior design by Exeter Premedia Services Private Ltd., Chennai, India

First published in 2021 by
Business Expert Press, LLC
222 East 46th Street, New York, NY 10017
www.businessexpertpress.com

ISBN-13: 978-1-95253-888-9 (paperback)
ISBN-13: 978-1-95253-890-2 (e-book)

Business Expert Press Economics and Public Policy Collection

Collection ISSN: 2163-761X (print)
Collection ISSN: 2163-7628 (electronic)

First edition: 2021

10 9 8 7 6 5 4 3 2 1

This book is dedicated to all those who love and support me.
Thank you for always being there for me.

Description

To successfully conclude a business conversation, negotiation skills and tactics are often not enough. If you enter a negotiation with fear, self-doubt or lack of conviction, you will not win, no matter how well tactically you have been trained. *Negotiation Booster* is a novel, synergistic approach leveraging the task-related aspects of a negotiation with the underlying emotional factors. It is the ultimate guide to winning negotiations by means of self-empowerment.

The distinguishing features of *Negotiation Booster* are as follows:

- It introduces an interdisciplinary approach to the topic of negotiation: the book explores fundamental negotiation tactics, communication, perception, and impression management techniques; the determinants of desired outcomes; and the issues that negotiators face internally and externally in the negotiation process;
- It equips the reader with practical tips on how to navigate around real-life challenges and avoid the most common mistakes that negotiators make;
- It provides a straightforward and user-friendly framework for strategic preparation and monitoring of progress (The Negotiation Matrix).

Target Audience: Business executives, international managers, lawyers, UN officials, and anyone who needs to negotiate professionally. This is a reference book for anyone who needs to boost their negotiation skills: academics, MBA and graduate students, business professionals, UN officials, international business managers, consultants, lawyers, salespeople, and marketing representatives.

Keywords

negotiation; bargaining power; self-empowerment; emotions management; perception management; success; ego; self-management

Contents

About the Author

Prof. Dr. Kasia Jagodzinska combines an academic career with international business advisory in the field of negotiations. She served as a senior adviser to the United Nations in Geneva, where she provided assistance in multistakeholder negotiations and conflict of interest management.

As a professor, she works with students from universities in Switzerland, France, Italy, and Poland. She holds a PhD in International Law and is multilingual and multicultural, having lived and worked in several countries.

She is the founder of *Negotiation Booster*, an innovative approach to business negotiations that leverages the task-related aspects of a negotiation with the underlying emotional factors.

In her role of international negotiation expert, she mentors and trains executives from the biggest corporations in Europe, Asia, the United States, and the Middle East. Working with business professionals from a wide array of industries and sectors gave her an in-depth understanding of the practical challenges they face in the interactions with their negotiation partners. Empowering others to succeed in negotiations is her passion.

Introduction

Negotiation Booster is the ultimate guide to winning negotiations by means of self-empowerment. It approaches the topic of negotiation from a new angle by bridging the strategic aspects with a self-management booster. The book equips the reader with technical skills and reinforces them with self-management strategies for successful negotiations.

The work is divided into two parts: the creative Part I (Negotiation Booster Primer) and the practical business examples Part II (Negotiation Booster Sealer). Jointly, they provide a comprehensive package of bulletproof negotiation tactics combined with tested tools for personal empowerment guaranteed to boost your bargaining power. As negotiation is an art as much as it is a science, *Negotiation Booster* draws from interdisciplinary sources. It equips the reader with cutting-edge insights on the key negotiation concepts, fundamental negotiation strategies, communication skills, perception and impression management techniques, the determinants of desired outcomes, and the issues that negotiators face internally and externally in the negotiation process. It is carefully designed to raise the reader's awareness of the impact of the most recent topics, such as intercultural sensitivity, virtual negotiations, and gender-related aspects.

All the creative chapters in Part I are enriched with a Further Reading section covering a total of more than 50 book reviews. Each of the proposed readings relates to the topic of the chapter and draws from a variety of fields, such as psychology, human resource management, communication, international business management, social studies, and more. The overview covers the classics, ancient, and modern-day thinkers. The Further Reading section provides a brief summary of each position along with key tips on its applicability for negotiators. This goldmine of condensed literature review provides a time-saving, straightforward source of reference that can be used to explore certain concepts in more depth to broaden your negotiation outlook.

Each chapter in Part I concludes with a compilation of the key takeaways for achieving success in negotiations. This format serves as a quick look-up tool while preparing for a negotiation or at any time during a negotiation to boost the chances of a successful outcome. Part II includes insights from international business practice. This part is the fruit of the authors' experiences as a negotiator, international trainer, and consultant for the United Nations in Geneva, Switzerland. It is a compilation of the experiences shared by business professionals of the biggest companies from Europe, Asia, the Middle East, and the United States. Part II equips the reader with practical tips on how to navigate around real-life challenges and avoid the most common mistakes that negotiators make.

Part III, the Negotiation Booster Implementor, offers a Negotiation Matrix—a user-friendly framework consisting of all the steps, phases, and elements of the negotiation process, along with a breakdown indication of what to pay attention to before, during, and after the negotiation. The Matrix can be used as a tool for preparation and monitoring progress.

The *Negotiation Booster* package is completed by the glossary of negotiation terms—a dictionary-format compilation of the key negotiation concepts that are covered throughout the book. It is designed for the reader's convenience as a summary of the material and a quick reference tool.

Finally, the reader will also benefit from a carefully selected list of references comprising negotiation classics, with indications of the subject matter that they address.

PART I
Negotiation Booster Primer

ONE of the essential skills of a master negotiator is the ability to read people in order to recognize their needs and anticipate their next move based on what they crave to achieve. The way a person behaves, both consciously and unconsciously, is very revealing. Decoding the real message behind their verbal and nonverbal communication is a valuable source of information, which can then be used as a powerful tool of influence. Sooner or later, we will all have to face a negotiation that may be life-changing for us, whether in a professional or personal setting. Its outcome will depend on how well we have trained ourselves in the art of negotiation. Practice makes perfect. It is, thus, helpful to develop the necessary skills on a continuous basis and not just *ad hoc* when we need to prepare for an upcoming negotiation.

If we are to trust the maxim: "We are what we do," then our choice of profession determines who we are and ultimately shapes how we view the world and how others perceive us. As a consequence of my professional occupation, people-watching has become somewhat of a full-time hobby for me. It is also an engaging pastime during the long hours of my travel in between the negotiation trainings and lectures I give around the globe. One of my most inspiring professors once said that life is a theater. He was not wrong. Only the setting changes, the actors are pretty much the same, no matter the geographical location. What strikes the most is the overwhelming level of estrangement from interactions with other people. Most people seem engaged in a relationship with their cell phones or computers, and themselves. Everyone is preoccupied with checking e-mails, chatting online, or whatever else activity they can think of with the use of the Internet. What people lack in interpersonal relations they compensate for with concentration on themselves.

Acts of self-admiration seem a sign of our times. I have frequently witnessed people acting like hermits among others, but at the same time, fully devoted to taking pictures of themselves—the so-called *selfies*. These selfies are then posted on Instagram, Facebook, or any other social network and shared with the rest of the world. It is as if people suddenly become online exhibitionists. The development of technology has created a kingdom where the ego can live and strive. As I pondered about all this, the term *selfie generation* came to my mind. It depicts a generation of self-oriented individuals governed by the need to exhibit their lifestyle, social status, achievements, activities, and ultimately, to feed their egos. Their distinguishing insignia is a selfie stick.

How does this self-concentration translate into modern business practice, specifically what are the implications for negotiations? More importantly, how can it be directed toward more productive aims? The spotlight on the self is not necessarily a bad thing, depending on where its beam is directed. In fact, the *I-focus* can be approached as a source of self-discovery and self-empowerment that may reinforce the relations with other people. More importantly, it shows us that success in any professional or personal endeavor starts not with technical prowess, but rather the human element.

To successfully conclude a business transaction, negotiation skills and tactics are often not enough. The importance of self-management, effective interpersonal communication, perception management, persuasion tactics, and reading others are the critical skills in boosting your negotiation power. If you enter a negotiation with fear, self-doubt, or lack of conviction, you will not win, no matter how well tactically you have been trained.

Negotiation Booster will equip you with the self-management toolkit that will allow you to tame emotions, ego, and stress in a negotiation. It will help you develop strategies for thriving in negotiations by means of directional self-management and personal empowerment. Consequently, I am addressing it to all those whose emotions, stress, and ego have gotten in the way of successful deal-making and for those who have to negotiate with people whose self is larger than life, or the so often called *difficult people*.

CHAPTER 1

Ego-tiation is the New Negotiation

Negotiation is a fairly formalized process between two parties trying to find an agreement regarding the distribution of a limited resource. This sounds reasonably straightforward, doesn't it? Why then is there so much commotion around the whole concept? Why do so many people feel stressed about negotiating and seek training, assistance, and guidance (judging by the volume of academic literature in the field and numerous number one bestsellers sold in millions of copies all over the world)? Moreover, why do so many negotiations go astray, leaving the participants with crumbs instead of the actual cake they were hoping to share?

These were the questions that incessantly lit up in my head during the negotiation sessions I took part in. They were also reflected in the experiences that my executives shared with me during our negotiation trainings. Still haunted by the dilemma, I was in the middle of one of my negotiation sessions when the revelation suddenly hit me. I was witnessing a power struggle between two super achievers who were trying to negotiate an agreement for the pharmaceutical companies they were representing. They certainly put on a great show. I was mesmerized to the degree that I was unconsciously applying the theoretical principles to what I was seeing. My mind had to tick the boxes and find a bridge between practice and theory. At first sight, everything seemed to fall into place: it was obvious which preparation patterns have been applied, there was awareness of the fundamental concepts, such as the opening offer, BATNA (best alternative to a negotiated agreement), ZOPA (zone of possible agreement), the chilling and boomerang effect, the basic negotiation techniques were being applied and the fundamental principles respected.

The tactical lenses were fogging my analytical capacity. I then realized that there was one element that I had not paid enough attention to until now. No longer was I witnessing a negotiation, it was an ego-tiation! The process was driven by an inordinate need for recognition and approval; it was a hunger game of the ego for both executives. However, it was clear that while the egos were taking over, the chances for the task accomplishment were getting slimmer.

Each negotiation consists of the task and the relationship-oriented aspects. For long-lasting agreements, there needs to be a balance between the task and the relationship between the parties.

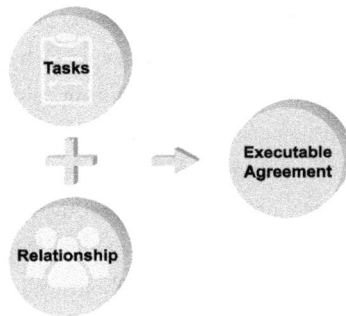

Figure 1.1 The task and relationship equation for executable agreements

Focus on achieving the desired negotiation outcome (task) will not be sufficient for securing a durable business arrangement. Conversely, making concessions for the sake of preserving the relationship will only lead to disenchantment in the long term. Therefore, the nature of the transaction will tip the scale to either side of the equation. Culture is also a decisive factor. According to cross-cultural researcher E. Hall, representatives coming from low-context cultures will tend to place a higher value on the task rather than on the relationship, as opposed to members from high-context cultures. Furthermore, G. Hofstede's analysis of cultural dimensions shows that cultures with a higher masculinity factor will also be more likely to place task before relationship.[1]

---

[1] The impact of cultural differences on negotiation and the theories of culture are presented in more detail in Chapter 15: The Impact of Culture on Negotiation.

At the individual level, once the ego takes over, it will usually drive the interaction more strongly toward unilateral goal attainment. The negotiation then turns into an ego-tiation. While the ego primarily takes over the reins on the individual level, it inevitably affects the dynamic between both parties.

The traditional approach views negotiation as a system of interdependency between the two parties interested in closing a transaction. One needs the other to achieve their negotiation objective. As shown in Figure 1.1, the focus can be either on the task at hand or the relationship part; ideally, it should be a combo package. Each party has their own agenda, which is driven by their specific interests. Interests are the shadow behind the position expressed by the negotiators, the ulterior motives. From the perspective of the negotiation environment, these interests are common, different, or conflicting. On the tactical level, these threefold interests need to be addressed in order for the parties to reach an agreement.

There is a second set of interests hidden below the waterline, those that operate on the individualistic level. Roger Fisher and Daniel Shapiro pointed out that each individual is steered by five principal interests: appreciation (sense of recognition or being understood), affiliation (sense of connectedness and belonging), autonomy (freedom to make decisions and take action), status (own standing in comparison to the standing of the other person), and role (a job position and associated tasks).

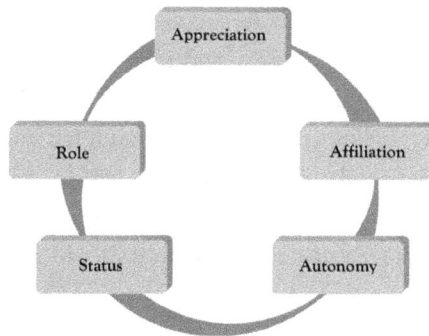

Figure 1.2 The five principal interests[2]

---

[2] Adapted from: Fisher, Roger, and Daniel Shapiro. Beyond Reason. Using Emotions as You Negotiate. London: Penguin Books, 2005.

The task versus relationship equation can best be explained with reference to game theory, a strategic reasoning approach that provides its user with the most optimal choice. Before deciding on a course of action, one party considers all of their opponent's possible decisions and tries to anticipate what the most probable one will be. Numbers are then attributed to each possible decision, from the most to the least desired outcome. One then chooses their best outcome depending on the anticipated choices of the opponent. The most known example is the Prisoner's Dilemma. Consider the following scenario: A and B get arrested and taken to the police station where they are separated in two different rooms. Each one is informed that if they confess, they will both spend only one year in prison. If one confesses and the other does not, the one who confessed will be released and the other will be sentenced to ten years. If both refuse to confess, then each will get five years in prison. The tricky part is that they cannot communicate between themselves in order to make the decision…

The role of an effective negotiator is to anticipate and uncover which interest is the directional force governing the actions of their counterpart. In other words, what lies at the core of their behavior? The opening offer, the position, and demands all flow from these interests. Very often, people will stubbornly defend their rigid positions because one of their core interests is not met or they feel that it is threatened. Loss aversion is a very strong motivational factor. In such moments, the ego takes the steer. If you want to succeed in a negotiation, learn how to identify what people really crave, and then find a creative way to give it to them without compromising on your own negotiation goals. Your negotiation partners will never forget how good it felt to do business with you, how well understood and respected they felt.

Keep in mind for your next negotiation that a good negotiator can hear the ego speak, a great negotiator can hear it whisper.

Key takeaways:
1. Balance the task and the relationship.
2. Identify what your negotiation partner wants, then find a creative way to give it to them.
3. Do not compromise on your own negotiation goals.
4. Separate reason from emotions.
5. Tame your ego, do not fight it.

Chapter 1: Further Reading

The following books will give you a broader perspective on how ego can affect your negotiation power:

1. **Sigmund Freud, *Group Psychology and the Analysis of the Ego***
   The absolute classic dating back to the 1920s that constitutes a timeless framework for understanding how groupthink occurs and what is the impact of ego on individual and collectivistic behaviors. Freud explains, among others, how the individual in a horde is influenced by group dynamics and how his or her mental activity is altered. He makes the distinction between rational and emotional stimulants. Ego falls in the latter category. A must-read for modern leaders and negotiators.

   Tip for negotiators: Control ego plays and prevents groupthink by limiting the number of people at the negotiation table.

2. **Katarzyna Jagodzinska, *Egotiation is the New Negotiation: The Concept of Negotiation Revisited***
   This article introduces a complete conceptualization, which grasps all the essential constituents of negotiation. It revisits the concept of negotiation and broadens it by the elusive element that, if not properly addressed, too often causes negotiations to fail: the ego factor. Consequently, this paper introduces the novel concept of ego-tiation. The new conceptual framework provides a straightforward and user-friendly reference that can be used when preparing for a negotiation or at any time during a negotiation to help improve the understanding of all the dynamics behind the negotiation process. Furthermore,

it unravels what negotiation really is based on the responses collected from a multicultural audience and aligns these results with the novel concept of negotiation.

> **Tip for negotiators:** Acknowledge the ego (yours and theirs) and keep it in check so that the negotiation does not transform into an ego-tiation.

3. **Ryan Holiday,** *Ego is the Enemy. The Fight to Master Our Greatest Opponent*

This work is true to the saying: Keep your friends close, but your enemies closer. The book is divided into three parts that reflect the steps of the journey toward accomplishing goals: aspire, success, failure. The twists and turns on the road are often caused by ego taking over the driver's seat.

> **Tip for negotiators:** Learn how to listen to your ego, and then become its master to avoid the failure part.

CHAPTER 2

Prime Yourself for Success

"IF I had eight hours to chop down a tree, I'd spend six sharpening my axe" (A. Lincoln). Preparation is the key to a successful negotiation or any other endeavor, for that matter. In order to prepare a bulletproof negotiation blueprint, tactical preparation needs to be combined with self-preparation. We will commence with the target. When defining the target, always start with a mental visualization of the maximum that you want to achieve. Your subconscious will find ways to attain that threshold. Although the walk-away amount should also be established, striving for the minimum will get you scraps at the negotiation table and beyond. A skilled counterpart will immediately sense when the minimum target has been reached and will try to anchor at that amount. The beauty of the matter is that nobody can set the limit of what you want to achieve, except for you.

Success comes only to those who dream big and find ways to make it happen. People respect boldness much more than cowardice. They flock toward those who are surrounded by an aura of confidence, nonchalance, and success. It is an irresistible mixture. Carry yourself like a winner and others will treat you like one. Weakness is associated with failure. Therefore, you might have to fake it until you make it. The first spectator you will need to convince is yourself, only then will the act be externally perceived as credible. Seduce your own mind first by selling it wonderful dreams.

A technique that works well is creating anticipatory emotions that have strong motivational power in goal attainment. Imagine how it would feel to already have achieved your desired outcome. Visualize the attributes of success, ignite the positive thoughts, and allow them to flow through your mind until you can almost grasp them. If executed properly, this visualization will create emotions that feel the same as the ones you experience in real-life business situations. There is no going back once you have had a taste of success, even if imaginary. At the negotiation table, you will not want to settle for less than what you envisioned. It would feel like a betrayal on your own mind.

Be specific and clear in relation to your objective in the negotiation. If you do not know what you want to achieve, it means you are not ready to take a seat at the negotiation table. Keep your eyes on the prize from the beginning, in order not to develop the habit of deviating from what you want to obtain. Do not create a precedence of compromising with yourself. Avoid an attachment to the past and negatively worded or wishy-washy (vague, general) targets. They are not specific enough and can collapse like a house of cards under the pressure of a negotiation; you need a clear roadmap that will lead you closer to your objective.

Once the target has been defined and the objective set, it is time for the design of the negotiation schedule and the choice of strategy that will lead you toward your desired negotiation outcome. Be the one who proposes the negotiation curriculum, sends out the invitation and, if possible, chooses the location for the meeting. It will allow you to set the stage as well as the tone for your future interactions. This must be done in a respectful and non-imposing manner so that the other party does not become defensive. You nonetheless take over the reins from the beginning.

This preparation blueprint might suggest that there is no place for flexibility in the process. Quite the contrary, a negotiation is like a journey. What you should know is that you want to get from point A to B, but you never know what adventures you will encounter during your journey. Therefore, a savvy negotiator will leave a margin of flexibility for the unexpected, in order to avoid being destabilized emotionally when things do not go strictly according to plan. The best approach is that of an enthusiastic traveler who enjoys the negotiation journey as much as reaching the agreement.

Flexibility aside, an important factor to keep in mind is that the majority of the decisions should be taken at the preparation phase. The brain is structured in such a way that when the external trigger enters it, we first feel (the amygdala responds), and only then we think. Contrary to what we would like to believe, the human is an emotional being, rather than a rational one. Good decisions can only be made based on the premise of reason, not emotions. The preparation phase is the moment that the emotional investment is at its lowest and emotions are fairly stable. Therefore, reason can rule uninterrupted. The only interaction is with oneself. Once the negotiation starts, external pressure will appear, and the stress levels will inevitably increase. Under these circumstances, it takes a lot of self-control and a strong prenegotiation mental priming to avoid being derailed from the negotiation goal.

Key takeaways:
1. Always try to strive for the maximum objective.
2. Have high expectations for yourself and your negotiation team.
3. Set a clear, precise, and future-oriented target.
4. Take leadership of the negotiation.
5. Make most of the decisions at the preparation phase.
6. Avoid setting yourself up for failure.

Chapter 2: Further Reading

Among the numerous studies on the topic of priming yourself for success, start with the following kickoff package:

1. **Napoleon Hill, *Think and Grow Rich***

   One of the landmarks in the field of moneymaking secrets. Far from black magic, it is the result of interviews with over 500 most successful entrepreneurs of Hill's time. This approach allowed the author to identify what are some of the prerequisites of prosperity. The common denominator turned out to be self-empowerment. It consists of two elements: the metaphysical—the power of the thought, desire, faith (visualizing the desired goal), autosuggestion, and imagination; and the physical—planning, decision-making, persistence, and directed drive. The main conclusion is that vision without action is wishful thinking.

   Tip for negotiators: Prime your mind for success and then take the necessary action to achieve it.

2. **Megyn Kelly,** *Settle for More*

A personal and authentic memoir of a news anchor who became known for standing her ground in the feud with Donald Trump. Kelly goes by the motto emblazoned on one of her sweatshirts: I want it all. She achieved success both in the professional and personal arena. Her recipe for affluence: once you change yourself for the better, better things will start coming your way. Settle for more—the *more* starts with yourself.

> **Tip for negotiators:** Nobody can set the limit of what you want to achieve, except for you.

3. **Jean-François Manzoni, Jean-Louis Barsoux,** *The Set-Up-To-Fail Syndrome. Overcoming the Undertow of Expectations*

A business-oriented study on confirmation bias, labels, and other perceptual pitfalls, which shows how bosses' behavior changes depending on whether they perceive the employee as a weak or strong performer. It refers to the Pygmalion effect—the phenomenon whereby high expectations bring high results, and the Golem effect—when low expectations yield weak returns. The main conclusion is that bosses can create their own poor performers.

> **Tip for negotiators:** Avoid the set-up-to-fail syndrome for yourself, never level down in your mind. Set the bar high and you will achieve success.

CHAPTER 3

Opening Offer: The Anchoring Effect

THE opening offer that you present to your counterpart will serve as an anchor for the whole negotiation process. It has a powerful framing effect and will serve as the benchmark for subsequent monetary and nonfinancial arrangements. The opening offer is like an invitation to dance. It is a subtle art that relies heavily on persuasion. However, to persuade at the moment that you need to ask for something is a moment too late.

In order to avoid the anchor from pulling you down, it is critical to carefully consider how to open. Similar to first impressions, there will never be a second chance to make a good first offer. The ideal opening offer should be as close as possible to the other party's barely acceptable terms. Making a ridiculous offer may lead to the boomerang or the chilling effect. The boomerang effect is when your negotiation partner considers your offer as too high and throws back an equally outrageous offer at you just for the sake of reciprocity. It is difficult to structure a constructive dynamic after such an unfortunate beginning. The parties risk entering into an ego struggle, which will divert attention from the merits of the discussion. The boomerang effect places the task part of the negotiation in jeopardy.

In turn, the chilling effect adversely affects the relationship. As the name itself suggests, the chilling effect happens when our counterpart loses interest in the negotiation at the outset. Their perception is that we are not negotiating in good faith. Nobody likes to feel manipulated or taken for a fool. Your role in a negotiation is to put your counterparts' ego at ease. This will lower their defenses and make them more open to future cooperation.

The ideal opening offer is, therefore, more than just a monetary value assessment; it is the first step to bridging the task and the relationship aspects of the negotiation. Many negotiations do not take off because the opening offers keep them grounded. In order to come up with a good opening, you need to gather internal and external intelligence. Equip yourself with as much information as possible about your counterpart: their ambitions, expectations, limitations, financial constraints, their pain threshold, and any personal circumstances that may have an impact on their decisions. The second part is the analysis of the external factors of the environment within which your counterpart operates: the state of the economy, political patterns, standards of business practice, trade customs, similar past transactions, market trends, and so on.

Once you have gathered sufficient information, it is time for the big question: who should open first? Before this decision is made, the advantages and disadvantages need to be taken into consideration. The obvious danger of opening first is that you might ask for less than the other party would have been ready to give. Ironically, there is nothing worse than a first offer that is immediately accepted. Instead of the feeling of victory, we will instead wonder whether we have not asked for too little. This is a precious lesson if you switch the dynamic around. Even if you consider that your counterpart has made you a great first offer, put up a little fight before accepting it. Approach it with a cool demeanor and be a long-term visionary. Use it as an opportunity to ask for concessions in the next stages of the negotiation. Send a signal that you reluctantly accept, but you will want something in return. The risk of asking for too little can be mitigated by a thoroughly conducted internal and external analysis. "Fail to prepare and you prepare for failure" (B. Franklin).

Allowing your counterpart to open first will trigger the anchoring effect, which will only work to your disadvantage. The subconscious is an inescapable force. You will inevitably find yourself entering the negotiation within the limits set forth by your counterpart. Their offer will serve as a reference point around which you structure yours. We are social beings, and as such, to some extent, we are used to accepting external constraints and viewing them as legitimate reality. Most people fear what others will think of them, they do not want to be labeled as greedy, irrational, or simply impolite.

For example, imagine that you are negotiating your fee for providing a given service. You are not sure how to open, perhaps you are (too) eager to close the deal, and you might lack market knowledge, experience, or conviction in your own value. It may be that putting a price tag on your own services makes you uncomfortable. The business prospect looks promising, and you feel like you have hit it off. You decide to ask the other party how much they would be willing to pay for such services. They give you the range of what they usually offer. At this point, you will oscillate around the values that *they* have provided.

The only time that you can allow yourself to wait for the opening offer is when the stakes are low. Another possibility is when a particular negotiation is not that important to you, and you just want to test the waters, for example, you are gathering offers from multiple other providers. Another occasion is when you want to put the relationship to the test and see how much the other party values you and what business etiquette they follow.

The opening offer should never be a cold call. If you want to increase the chances of your offer being accepted, design the stage well before the offer itself appears on the table. Water the soil before you plant the seeds. Set high standards by references to prestigious companies you have done deals with and big players with whom you would like to be associated, choose top-notch business locations for your meeting, use high-quality marketing materials, make sure you and your team looks and acts to the highest professional standards. You might even go as far as mentioning a number from a past transaction, make it seem like a slip of the tongue, do not dwell on it. Your counterpart will subconsciously register all these attributes of success and will treat you accordingly.

Your job is not done yet. Now that the stage is set, it is time to make your offer the object of desire so that its allure does not fade when competition steps in. A bare opening offer will quickly lose its appeal, unless it is garmented properly. A skilled negotiator knows how to uncover the hidden needs of their partner and make them believe that only their offer can satisfy them. Lure your negotiation partner in by appealing to their tastes, then send them off on a pursuit after your offer. Make it seem like it can be taken away. All the while remember that you set the value for yourself first. If you want to play big, anchor like a winner.

Key takeaways:
1. Whenever possible, open first.
2. Equip yourself with information about the acceptability threshold of your partner.
3. Avoid the boomerang and chilling effect.
4. Make your offer the object of desire.
5. Pre-suade before you persuade.
6. Anchor like a winner to be a winner.

Chapter 3: Further Reading

For more information on how to preset the stage to win your negotiations, you may be interested in the following positions:

1. **Robert Cialdini, *Pre-Suasion. A Revolutionary Way to Influence and Persuade***

   A compilation of the tools of social influence with a twist: the focus is on the moments before the tool comes in handy. The author presents the primers that will increase the likelihood of winning people over.

   Tip for negotiators: Adapt the process of pre-suasion consisting of six concepts: reciprocation (people treat others the way they are treated), liking (linked to the principle of similarity), social proof (doing something because others are doing it), authority (trustworthiness by means of being an authority figure), scarcity (wanting more of what we can have less of), and consistency (cohesion with existing commitments) in your negotiations.

2. **Robert Greene, *The Art of Seduction***

   The physical act of sex is an activity of the body, and as such, it quickly tends to lose its appeal. Seduction is an activity of the mind; its effects are much more powerful and far more dangerous. Seduction primarily relies on creating a desire not for the physical, but for something greater: a fantasy. As such, it is the ultimate tool of power and persuasion. A skilled seducer knows how to uncover the hidden needs of their victim and make them believe that only they can satisfy them. How different is this from negotiation?

   Tip for negotiators: Make your offer irresistible.

3. **Kevin Dutton, *Flipnosis. The Art of Split-Second Persuasion***

A refreshing perspective on the science of persuasion that cracks the code of persuasion. A witty, surprising study of human nature and the art of social influence. The book provides valuable insights into what makes people prone to mental stimulation. The author provides a lethal cocktail of influence consisting of five ingredients: flipnosis, simplicity, perceived self-interest, confidence, and empathy (Page 13).

Tip for negotiators: Mix it to your liking and serve it to your negotiation partner to warm them up to your opening offer.

CHAPTER 4

On Alternatives: We Won the Lottery!

HAVE you ever failed at something that you thought was the most important thing for you to achieve or have at that point in your life? If so, you probably tormented yourself by what you could have done better and how you would have acted differently if you could turn back time and get a second chance. Sometimes, a second opportunity comes along, and you can have what you once thought you dreamed of. When it is attainable, suddenly, it becomes less desirable. You may even find that you do not want it anymore and that, somehow, it has lost its appeal. Remember how that revelation felt so that you can use its power when you create alternatives for your next negotiation.

In a negotiation, the two fundamental concepts are ZOPA and BATNA. They will be explained from two angles: the technical one and the self-empowering one. ZOPA is the zone of possible agreement. It is a numerical representation of the overlap between the most that the buyer is willing to pay and the minimum that the seller is willing to accept.

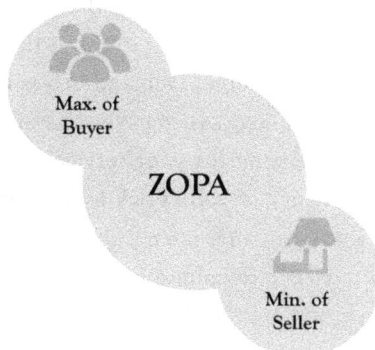

Max. of
Buyer

ZOPA

Min. of
Seller

Figure 4.3 Zone of possible agreement (ZOPA)

One of your tasks is to identify what that number is for your negotiation partner. The question is, what happens when there is no financial overlap, in other words, when the gap in money terms is insurmountable? Those who will nonetheless want to close the transaction will turn toward creative options. Creating options requires considering what are the elements in the negotiation that have a high cost for you, but which constitute a lower cost for your negotiation partner. For example, if you want to buy a car and you and the car dealer do not have a ZOPA, you should consider the global cost of the car and not just the selling price. Then, identify those constituents that are an item of expenditure for you, but are not necessarily a big cost item for the car dealer, such as servicing, winter tires storage, and so on. Lead the negotiation forward by trading those elements to minimize the monetary gap. A good car dealer will most likely engage in that negotiation, because they will see a potential for a long-term relationship. If the negotiation dynamic and outcome are satisfactory, chances are they have just won themselves a loyal customer. This approach will not work in a one-time transaction, such as the sale of a used car. It is worth pointing out that creative options are designed inside the negotiation, that is, when both parties still want to close a particular deal.

BATNA is an acronym that depicts the best alternative to a negotiated agreement. The keyword here is alternative. This means that a BATNA is outside of the negotiation, as opposed to options. It is your fallback position when an agreement in a specific situation with a particular partner cannot be reached.

BATNA is like your secret; you imply that you have one to your counterpart, but you do not confess what it is. It is that mystical aura that makes your offering more desirable. Demand drives demand. The worst possible signal that you can send is that you do not have alternatives, other people are not competing for your services, your expertise, time, or your product. The beauty of a BATNA is that you craft it yourself. Remember, there is always an alternative. One of the deadliest mistakes that you can possibly make is to enter a negotiation with a mindset that this is the only chance, the only option, there is nothing beyond, this is it or nothing. Think about it logically, how many life situations leave you with no other alternative?

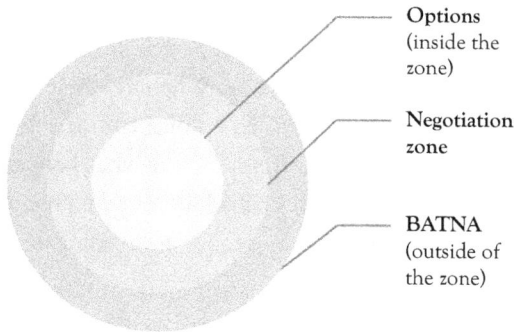

Options
(inside the
zone)

Negotiation
zone

BATNA
(outside of
the zone)

Figure 4.4 Best alternative to a negotiated agreement (BATNA)

To illustrate the power of alternatives, I will refer to the parable of the man who won (or so he thought) the lottery. This particular man lost his job. The economy was at a standstill, and there were few job openings. He was not completely unprepared for a career change. To make things worse, he had a family to support, a mortgage on the house, as well as a few other financial obligations toward the bank. The man started interviewing for the few jobs that he could find, which fit his skillset and more or less corresponded to his expectations. Meeting after meeting, he was rejected by the recruiters. At that point, not only his financial resources were getting slimmer, but his self-esteem and morale were lower with each unsuccessful attempt. Soon, desperation became his trademark in the interviews. He got to the point where he turned to luck as his final straw, and started purchasing lottery tickets. This was surprising even to him, as he always had an internal locus of control. He believed that he is the maker of his own destiny, that luck is something you work for.

His wife was witnessing all this with growing fear, but she never let him see her own concern. One day, as he was putting on his suit for yet another encounter with the head of the human resources (HR) department of one of the companies on his list, she was watching him. He looked like the embodiment of failure. His entire body language had changed. The command presence he once had was gone. He seemed smaller and weaker physically, and internally, he was lacking motivation and confidence. She knew that the interviewer would see it too. Nobody would offer him a job at this point. There needed to be something that she could do to change this. As usual, he kissed her goodbye and got on the train to attempt yet another meeting. When he was just about to enter the meeting room, she called him. In a voice simmering with joy and excitement, she shrieked: "You will not believe what happened. Darling, we won the lottery!" She told him she had just checked the numbers from last night, and that they got a hit. She told him to come home, as they no longer needed that job.

Overwhelmed by this great news, he felt as if suddenly the weight of the world had been lifted off his shoulders. He considered going straight back home, but then thought that if he already made the trip, he might as well get the meeting over with out of courtesy for the time of the interviewer. He walked into the room with an aura of confidence. That evening when he came back home, he took his wife in his arms and said to her: "We have two things to celebrate." To his surprise, she replied that actually there was only one—his new job offer.

The story shows that letting go often decreases resistance and creates new opportunities that you did not notice while obsessing over a perceived failure. The key to boosting your negotiation power is twofold. On the technical level, you need to create alternatives. You either identify existing ones or craft alternative courses of action, should the negotiation fail. Ask yourself what you can and will do if that happens, then strengthen that substitute. Accept it as an equally exciting possibility. If you do not feel that way, it means the alternative is not yet strong enough. At the same time, you need to tend to the underlying force—your inner power flowing from having an alternative. Win the lottery in your own mind and see how empowered that makes you feel.

Key takeaways:
1. Identify what is the maximum that you are willing to offer.
2. Identify what is the minimum that your negotiation partner is willing to accept.
3. Design creative options to bridge the financial overlap between those two values.
4. Create and strengthen your alternatives.
5. Remember that there is always an alternative.
6. Allow the existence of alternatives to empower you.

Chapter 4: Further Reading

The following selections will strengthen your belief that there are always alternative choices in life:

1. **Sheryl Sandberg, Adam Grant, *Option B. Facing Adversity, Building Resilience and Finding Joy.***

   How do you rebuild your life after you lose someone who is like your rock? This is what Sandberg had to do when her beloved husband passed away during their vacation in Mexico. The book starts with a retrospect to this traumatic event and takes the author through the phases of grief toward a vision of a brighter future filled with hopes of love and laughter anew. This personal experience is a testimony to the fact that even in the face of adversity, it is possible to persevere by crafting self-confidence, building strength, and resilience.

   Tip for negotiators: If there exists an option B in the ultimate test of life (and death), then there surely are alternatives in any other human endeavor.

2. **Jia Jang, *Rejection Proof. How to Beat Fear and Become Invincible***

   The ability to deal with rejection is one of the skills that a negotiator needs to master in order to succeed. The fear of failure often translates into not trying all. In extreme cases, it can paralyze to the verge of inaction. Such was the case of the author. While still in college, Jang had an idea for an innovative product that he wanted to introduce to the market. He presented the concept to his uncle, for whom he had high regard. To his great disappointment, his uncle criticized the project severely. This experience was so painful that Jang abandoned his entrepreneurial dream for many years to come.

   However, the dream was always lurking in the back of his mind. The problem was that the critique that he received turned into a full-blown phobia of rejection. To overcome it, Jang set out on a 100-day mission during which he deliberately sought out situations for (presumably) sure-shot social rejection. One of the experiments was his request to pilot an aircraft. His findings were eye-opening:

rejection is just a number (at some point, someone, somewhere will say yes), so never give up.

    Tip for negotiators: There is always an alternative to the initial proposal. View rejection as an opportunity to improve: your attitude, your offer, your strategy, and your negotiation approach.

3. **Harvey Mackay, *Dig Your Well Before You're Thirsty***

In general, this is a book on the power of networking, which is undeniably one of the top business skills. In essence, it is a collection of savvy business tips on building and expanding your contact list. The support of personal connections can open many doors under one condition: you prepare the ground before you actually need the backing.

My favorite maxim: "Prepare to win. Then prepare to dazzle" (Page 35).

    Tip for negotiators: Craft alternatives well before the negotiation. Anything later than that will be an act of damage control that will lessen your bargaining power.

CHAPTER 5

Manage Perception to Win Negotiations

To win your negotiation partner over, you need to first understand how they perceive reality. The advantage is twofold. Firstly, this will allow you to operate on their perceptual level, and secondly, you can design what you want them to see. A fundamental element of perception management is framing. A frame is the individual lens through which people see the world, which affects how they organize information, evaluate situations, and what actions they consequently take. Because of a spectrum of individual differences, backgrounds, life experiences, expectations, motives, wants, and fears, each person frames reality in a distinctive way. Although each individual has a unique story that shaped who they are and how they perceive and react to certain situations, the process is governed by a framework of collectivist symbols.

In a negotiation, it is not uncommon that the two parties notice different things based on the information they selectively focus on. Interpretations made on the basis of selective screening are impacted by past experiences, as well as by the application of implicit moral rules, standards of behavior, and business conduct. They may also depend on how the information itself is presented. Quite often, people develop self-serving biased perceptions: they fixate on what they want to believe and reject all information that does not fulfill this purpose. Not surprisingly, the conclusions then reached are one-sided and mirror one party's self-interest only; hardly the best environment for an executable agreement.

The traditional approach to perception management in negotiation implies that there are at least two parties whose perceptions differ. These divergences then shape the negotiation dynamics. This is accurate only in part. It lacks the own, personal story of each party: their observation of the situational context, their interpretation, and their own conclusions. This is what sets the wheels of the perceptual process into motion and alters not only one's own story, but also the story (and behavior) of the person with whom they are dealing with.

More importantly, at the outset, perception in negotiation does not require the involvement of the parties. It starts on the individual level. Initial one-sided perception (the perception one has in their own mind) frames reality and evokes certain emotions, which are then reflected in behavior. The other party perceives the behavioral signal and reacts accordingly to this framing (see Figure 5.5). Managing one's own perception first can, thus, be used as a powerful tool of influence.

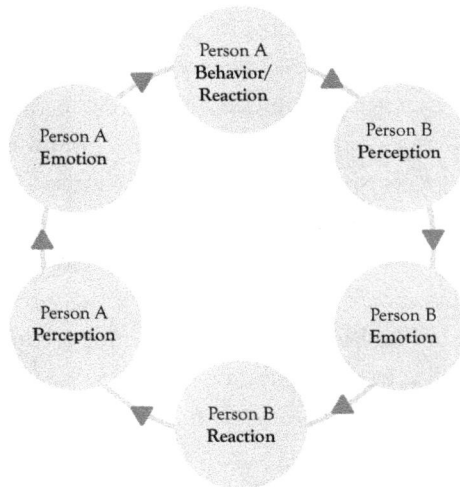

Person A
Behavior/
Reaction

Person B
Perception

Person A
Emotion

Person B
Emotion

Person A
Perception

Person B
Reaction

Figure 5.5 The mechanism of perception management

In an era of technology overload, we become immune to the constant flow of news bombarding us from all angles and channel our attention to the task at hand. To remain sane, the brain has to manage the data. It does so by selective screening—filtering of information in order to deal only with the most important matters. Selective screening is governed by external and internal factors. The former are characteristics of the person being perceived, and the latter are characteristics of the perceiver. Person perception is a three-dimensional process by which the individual attributes characteristics or traits to other people. It is shaped by the external and internal factors, as well as the situation or context within which perception takes place. External features of the perceived are, among others, age, posture, gender, voice quality, facial expressions, attributes of power, social status, role, and so on. These are the elements we immediately notice about the other person, and that send us a strong, albeit unconscious signal. Based on our observations, we make preliminary judgments, categorize the person and make plans about how to deal with them, which negotiation strategy to adopt, and which tactics to use.

By means of a simplified example, we may view a smartly dressed executive in their mid-40s, with a straight posture and a hard look in their eyes, speaking in a confident and strong voice as someone who might be a seasoned and no-nonsense negotiator. They have command presence—the aura of authority. People make judgments based on their perceptions, which are, to a large extent, based on how you look and behave. You should, therefore, control how you want your negotiation partner to see you. Various experiments supported by real-life observations show that people are easily fooled by appearances, we are programmed by society to react to symbols of authority. The brain often operates on autopilot, the so-called System 1.

For example, dressing a person up as a doctor and having them conduct a health survey is enough for some people to agree to answer personal questions. Similarly, someone who presents themselves as an *expert* in a negotiation meeting has the other members on alert, as they assume that they are dealing with a person with elevated expertise that they themselves might be lacking.

Characteristics of the perceiver fall into the following three categories: personality, learning, and inner drive. These internal features predetermine how one interprets reality based on his or her present state of being, as well as past similar experiences, which have a bearing on the way the individual will behave in similar future circumstances. This phenomenon is referred to as the system of pertinence of an individual. With reference to the selfie generation, it can best be described as a snapshot of a person's life at a given moment. Such a photograph would depict all the preoccupations, motivations, dreams, fears, joys, hopes, and so forth, linked to the past that shape how the person sees himself or herself, others, and the world at a given moment.

In relation to negotiation, it is vital to pay adequate attention to recognizing individual differences (the internal factors) and their effect on how the person with whom we are dealing with views the environment (the translation into external factors). This has never been easier than now, when many people willingly exhibit their private lives for the whole world to see. Equip yourself with information about your negotiation partner. We are each our own favorite topic. Few can resist the temptation of talking about themselves. By doing so, your counterpart will reveal precious tips on what makes them click. Understanding your negotiation partners' system of pertinence lowers their defenses and makes it easier for you to steer the negotiation toward your goal.

The last element forming the perceptual puzzle is the situation or context within which perception takes place. Just as you should govern how the other party perceives you, you should also tend to the framing of the negotiation setting. Whenever possible, be the one who decides where the meeting will be taking place and at what time. People are more receptive on certain days of the week and times of the day. Mondays and Fridays are not the best days, just as before lunchtime is not a good time for productive negotiations. Always manage the design of the meeting room according to the impression you want to make. Direct the spotlight on what you want the other party to see and block out the rest.

Key takeaways:
1. Manage the perception you have of yourself first.
2. Craft and control how you want to be perceived externally.
3. Understand how your partner perceives reality.
4. Selectively screen their attention to your objective.
5. Frame the negotiation setting to the effect you want to make.

Chapter 5: Further Reading

To better comprehend how the perception process works and how you can use this knowledge to affect the behavior of yourself and your negotiation partner, take a look at the following positions:

1. **Carl G. Jung,** *Man and His Symbols*

   The sentence from this book: "Perception is the only reality" reveals it all. This work is the result of Jung having interpreted at least 80,000 dreams of his patients that highlight individual tendencies. He found that on the whole, they seem to fall into a universally shared pattern. The book is a fascinating study about the unconscious element of the psyche, the process of individuation (precious insights for understanding ego development and maturity levels), and ancient myths and symbols that affect certain behaviors. Jung makes a distinction between the self—the totality of the psyche understood as the inner guiding factor, and the ego—a small part of the psyche that needs to give itself in to psyche in order for growth to occur.

   🤝 **Tip for negotiators:** A skilled negotiator needs to understand how all these elements: the symbols, the individual self, and the ego impact perception.

2. **Katarzyna Jagodzinska,** *How to Manage Perception to Win Negotiations*

   In this article, I point out that the way in which negotiators perceive themselves and how they feel can have a significant influence on the other party's perception of them. Consequently, the first step is taking command over the perception a person has of oneself, and then using this control to manage how others will perceive and act toward us. This realization is fundamental in breaking away from the mental constraints that too often cause people to fail in negotiations or impede their full potential.

   🤝 **Tip for negotiators:** By programing the mind into believing in your inner strength and not allowing others to sway this conviction, you can considerably increase your actual bargaining power.

3. **Tali Sharrot,** *The Influential Mind. What the Brain Reveals About Our Power to Change Others*

   A primer on persuasion offering an analysis of common behaviors grounded in scientific research. An extremely approachable and very relatable study. The author shares Jung's view that "perception is what matters, not objective reality" (Page 102). She takes the discussion one step further by linking perception management with behavioral change. Sharrot points out that the need for control drives human behavior. By allowing the other person the right to choose, you can lower their resistance and make them more open to cooperation. This is a valuable insight for negotiators.

Tip for negotiators: Power can be obtained by letting go (or making it seem so); the effect is there even if the sense of control is only illusionary—a perception (!)

CHAPTER 6

The Three-Dimensional (3D) Perception Model

THE three-dimensional (3D) perception model is a tool that negotiators can use in order to master the art of perceptual management in negotiation. The model comprises the trio of individual, relational, and situational perception. At the core of the 3D perception model lies the unique perception that each person makes, which starts the six-step process during which they observe, select, organize, interpret, and respond to a perceptual trigger that enters the brain.

This mechanism is governed by internal and external characteristics. Individual perception influences how others see and react to us. Consequently, it has a bearing on the relational element: the nature and the rules governing the relationship with the party we are dealing with. Individual and relational dynamics then define the approach of parties A and B to the negotiation object. The situational context is the continuum of all these elements reflected in the negotiation strategy, approach, tactics employed, and so on.

Over the years, I have applied the 3D perception model in my negotiations and have taught it to executives, students, and business professionals. Many have admitted that the model opened their eyes to certain dynamics, either caused by their own behavior or the conduct of the other party, which have, usually adversely, affected their bargaining power and the end result. The model made them realize what was the elusive element that was often causing their negotiations to go astray. *Post-factum* analysis of their negotiations in relation to the model allowed them to take command over the perceptual process and adjust their future negotiation approach accordingly. Furthermore, it has helped them raise awareness about the individual, relational, and situational perception elements that might come into play in any future negotiation.

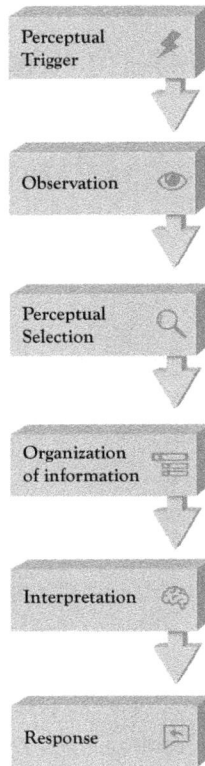

Figure 6.6 The perceptual process[3]

The most important realization drawn from the 3D perception model is that the starting point of perceptual selection, which determines the outcome of any negotiation, lies within. Each person can learn how to exercise command over their selective screening, for example, by focusing on boosting one's confidence and mental best alternative to a negotiated agreement (BATNA) while blocking out the background noise, such as anxiety, nervousness, self-questioning, and doubting one's bargaining power. A self-conscious attitude, inner stability, and aura of control will certainly not go unnoticed by the other party who will adjust their behavior accordingly. Researchers who study body language confirm that posture and nonverbal behavior shape who we are. Nonverbals not only

---

[3] Adapted from: Slocum, J.W., and D. Hellriegel. 2011. *Principles of Organizational Behavior*, Page 121, 13th ed. South-Western Cengage Learning.

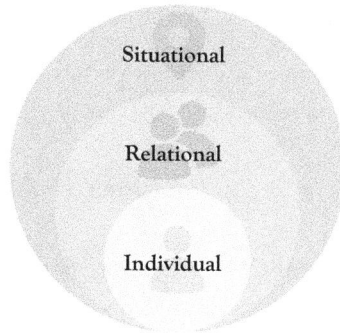

Situational

Relational

Individual

Figure 6.7 The 3D perception model

affect how you feel about yourself, but also how others see and react to you. Ultimately, it all comes down to creating an aura of power, first internally and then externally.

By now, we know that preparation is the condition *sine que non* of a successful negotiation. Most executives approach this too literally, they only focus on the technical aspects. A solid and comprehensive preparation package includes the management of the perceptual process of oneself as a means of influencing the perception of the other party. This is the pre-step of convincing the other party to our logic, which reflects our needs and interests. Adopting such an approach will help to navigate through any negotiation, be it with a *difficult* person or with a, presumably, much stronger opponent.

Key takeaways:
1. Take command over the individual, relational, and situational perception.
2. Create an aura of power internally and externally.
3. Base your power on what you can control.
4. Master the art of indirection.
5. Combine strategic preparation with perceptual management.

Chapter 6: Further Reading

The following books uncover a different perspective on how to craft the perception of yourself to your desired effect:

1. **Scott Adams, *Win Bigly. Persuasion in a World Where Facts Don't Matter***

   Known for creating the Dilbert comic series and having predicted Trump's win in the elections, Adams is far more than a political fortune-teller. He applies his training in the art of hypnosis, which is the ultimate form of mental persuasion, to universal life and business situations. The book is an intriguing, at times controversial, compilation of perception management and persuasion tips based on examples of the moguls from the political and business arena. What you can learn from them is that to become more influential in your negotiations, you should create two ways to win, no way to lose (Page 189).

   Tip for negotiators: Frame your mind for success and leave your counterpart no other option than reaching an agreement with you.

2. **Robert Greene, *The 48 Laws of Power***

   Greene is often referred to as the *Modern Machiavelli*, and in this book, the author lives up to that label. The book contains lessons from the most powerful historical figures and conveys the stories of individual, relational, and situational craftsmanship that led them to glory and success. The 48 laws cover planning, strategic preparation, creating options, time management, persuasion technics, and manipulation tricks to use and guard against. A fascinating and potentially dangerous toolkit if applied to the wrong means.

   Tip for negotiators: Step in the game of power by mastering the art of indirection.

3. **Niccolo Machiavelli, *The Prince***

   A treaty on the different kinds of states and how to conquer them. On the ulterior level, a study of power. The book contains both the technical (strategic) approach to warfare and the self-management aspects of what it takes to win and stay in power. Take Machiavelli's advice when establishing your power in negotiations: "A sensible man will base his power on what he controls, not on what others have freedom to choose" (Page 68).

Tip for negotiators: Rely primarily on your inner resources: "The only good, sure, lasting forms of defense are those based on yourself and your own strength" (Page 97).

CHAPTER 7

Impression Management: The Attribution Trap

ONE of the primary tasks of a negotiator is to persuade the other party to an agreement and to lead to a desired behavior. It is, thus, necessary to understand what causes behavioral change. The attribution process is the way that people make sense of the causes of their own and other's behavior. It consists of three elements: antecedents, attributions, and consequences. Antecedents are the factors internal to the perceiver, such as the amount of information he or she has about the other party and the overall situation, as well as the perceivers' needs and motives. Based on these factors, the perceiver makes attributions about the presumed cause of behavior of the person being perceived. The assigning of cause leads to consequences, which are reflected in certain feelings, behaviors, and related expectations.

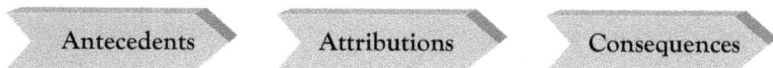

Antecedents   Attributions   Consequences

Figure 7.8 The attribution process[4]

The attribution process is highly subjective because it is primarily governed by the factors internal to the perceiver. For example, an experienced or well-trained negotiator will pay attention to much more detail than a novice might notice. Nonetheless, the margin of error in correctly comprehending and assessing the causes of behavior remains substantive. Achieving perceptual accuracy is a challenge in itself, because there are so many attribution traps that await, not to mention habits that can create patterns of behavior that are difficult to overcome. Similarity, contrast,

---

[4] Adapted from: Slocum, J.W., and D. Hellriegel. 2011. Principles of Organizational Behavior, Page 121, 13th ed. South-Western Cengage Learning.

or first-impression errors, may adversely affect the cause (attribution) and effect relationship (consequences). While it is inevitable (and often recommended) to filter the flow of information, excessive selective screening leads to perceptual defense, defined as hearing only what we want to hear. Studies have shown that the human brain processes positive events and data much more accurately than negative ones. This is why the tactic known as flattery is so dangerous; few people can resist the allure of having their egos stroked. The risk related to perceptual defense is that one might fail to grasp the broad picture when negotiating, especially when dealing with a party who can sweet talk us into a deal. As a safeguard, it is essential to carefully balance the good aspects with the less favorable ones.

Another common perceptual error is stereotyping—assuming that all members of a particular group share the same features, traits, or behaviors. In the era of internationalization of business affairs, not only is this offensive, but it also limits the ability to fully comprehend and craft creative solutions based on individual differences and resulting preferences. On the other hand, projection—an error consisting in assigning one's own traits to the other person—may equally cloud our judgment of the person with whom we are dealing with, which in turn may cause us to let our guard down, and in consequence, negatively impact the negotiation process. The similarity principle is one of the strongest universal social bonds. For example, a simple fact such as a negotiator's name starting with the same letter as the counterpart's can create a favorable inclination toward that person. This is not necessarily a bad thing, provided we are aware of its impact and can guard ourselves against the perceptual bias that it may create.

Quite an interesting perceptual mistake is the phenomenon referred to as the halo effect, which I call the *devil or angel impression*. It occurs when one either positive or negative characteristic dominates the way you *see* your negotiation partner. The way we perceive someone radiates through us and ultimately impacts our behavior toward our counterpart. If the dominant taste that we have is bitter, then we run the risk that our concern with the negativity may adversely affect the relational dynamics with the other party and ultimately ruin the whole situational framework. A positive halo effect is equally risky because it may make us more prone to giving in to unreasonable demands or making concessions based on pure sympathy rather than logic and fair standards.

Lastly, it is worth pointing out that we are creatures of habit. How we negotiate is often based on a habitual pattern of behavior. Your negotiation conduct is the result of three elements: the hereditary legacy (what you observed in your first socio-economic environment, your family), the corporate culture of your work environment that shaped your professional silhouette, and your trial-and-error approach, usually governed by your intuition. After each negotiation, debrief yourself on your performance. You will notice a pattern emerge. This is your negotiation habit. Now you can identify the specific areas you would like to improve in your future negotiations.

In order to avoid falling into one of the attribution traps, I recommend that you enter a negotiation with the awareness of the existence of perceptual biases that have an impact on you and your counterpart. Defend yourself against the temptation of succumbing to perceptual shortcuts and be wary of the impression management tactics that the other party may use to manipulate your perception.

Key takeaways:
1. Understand what drives behavioral change (yours and theirs).
2. Frequently check your perceptual accuracy.
3. Learn to spot and avoid impression errors.
4. Do not fall for flattery.
5. Create good negotiation habits.
6. Steer clear of perceptual shortcuts.

Chapter 7: Further Reading

While it is useful to know how the attribution process works, sometimes, the strongest impressions are made by breaking away from the expected norm. An element of novelty or surprise contrast against the familiar is a strong attention-getter. To find out more, you can refer to the following:

1. **Charles Duhigg, *The Power of Habit. Why We Do What We Do in Life and in Business***
   An eye-opening study that explains the habit loop—how habits are formed and how they can be changed. Habit is a three-step cycle consisting of the cue (e.g., feeling stressed), the routine (e.g., smoking a cigarette), and the reward (feeling less anxiety). The good news

is that any habitual behavior can be altered, provided the cue and the reward stay the same. In order to break an old habit (and perhaps replace it with a new one), you need to address the old craving. The trick is to change the routine that will satisfy that old thirst.

Tip for negotiators: Break down your negotiation habit into three steps. Keep the cue and the reward the same, and insert a new routine that will make your future negotiations healthier.

2. **Francesca Gino, *Rebel Talent. Why it Pays to Break the Rules at Work and in Life***

Attribution errors are essentially habitual mental shortcuts and routines, often embedded in a web referred to as rules. Negotiators, businesses, and societies function according to a predetermined set of acceptable standards of business and social conduct. It is much easier that way, but is it always efficient? Gino dares to disagree. She shows that in certain situations, it pays to challenge the rules and to create a new order.

Tip for negotiators: Be a rebel with a cause in your negotiations—do not break the rules for the sake of allowing your best impression of yourself shine through whatever you do. Stand out from the crowd and create your own standards of negotiation excellence.

3. **Joe Dispenza, *You are the Placebo. Making Your Mind Matter***

We often use the expression *think outside the box* in business meetings and negotiations. Have you ever stopped to wonder what is inside the box in order to step outside of it? For that matter, what is the box anyway? The term depicts the phenomenon related to neurorigidity. It is an ensemble of thoughts, emotions, and patterns of interpretation that follow a predetermined (habitual) path. In other words, the same thoughts equal the same feelings and lead to the same behaviors over and over again. Consequently, the brain develops a kind of finite neural signature. You recreate the same mental landscape every day. It is as if you were working only one muscle at the gym. Over time, your brain will limit itself to a specific neural framework—you are thinking in the box.

Tip for negotiators: Now that you know the limitations, expand the mental horizon in your negotiations by avoiding the attribution constraints. The added value—you will develop more neuroplasticity.

CHAPTER 8

On Profiling: Do Not Use a Gun for a Mosquito

IN order to steer the negotiator toward your desired outcome, you need to know who your counterpart is, what are their interests and motivation. The person behind the case will be the one with whom you will be dealing. To a large degree, the facts are only the scenery. Work the man, not the case, and you will succeed.

Equip yourself with the right tools: adapt your negotiation approach, style, language, and tactics to fit your counterpart. This tailor-made approach is referred to as profiling. This includes a 360-degree analysis of the type of negotiator you are dealing with, their personality traits, their ego maturity level, the sources of power they rely on, their communication style, and the culture prototype. A critical aspect is keeping your perception accuracy at check, and not allowing impression management techniques that may be used by the other party to fog your assessment. Take care also not to succumb to the allure of perceptual shortcuts, such as stereotyping, bias, first impressions, similarity or contrast errors, or the halo effect (a positive impression of a person that has a positive influence on your opinion in other areas).

Negotiation profiling is a three-step process, which consists of identification of the negotiation type, decision-making pattern, and reaction to stress.[5] There are two negotiation types: the rational and the emotional. The rational individual responds to laws, regulations, data, facts, figures, and numbers. In order to win them over, you will need to appeal to logic and refer to objective criteria. The emotional type depends on intuition, their sixth sense, perhaps even the occult, and as such is less predictable. The feelings you invoke are more important than the facts.

---

[5] Schranner, M. 2008. Costly Mistakes: The 7 Biggest Errors in Negotiations. Germany: Schranner.

When it comes to decision-making patterns, you will encounter the judging type and the perceiving type. The first is a fast implementer, an action-oriented, tick-the-list type of individual, typically a project manager or a salesperson. The latter is the slow implementer, a person who does not like to part with their decision. There is no use in pushing them, it will only make them more hesitant.

In stressful situations, there are two distinctive behavioral patterns: the fight or flight mechanism. For the fight type, attack is the best defense. Under pressure, this person will disrupt the communication by one-sided argument overkill, stubborn attachment to their rigid position, loud and aggressive behavior, or taking offense. The flight type is likely to retreat, close up to communication, give in, or become passive.

The next element in your profiling package is the personality assessment. The most popular classification that you can refer to is the Big Five Personality Test, which distinguishes the following dimensions of personality: openness, conscientiousness (attention to detail), agreeableness, extraversion, and neuroticism (emotionalism). Pay attention to the potential existence of poisonous personality features, known as the dark triad: narcissism, Machiavellianism (depicting manipulative, self-centered, ethically dubious behaviors), and forms of psychopathy. The individuals who display such traits of character are often labeled as *difficult people* or emotional vampires.

A variation of the dark triad is the God complex, a situation in which the ego becomes overinflated as a result of a successful professional career. The individual considers themselves as having achieved divine status in their respective field of knowledge, and consequently perceives themselves as superior to others. You should pay attention to the ego maturity level of your counterpart. Are they addicted to praise and flattery? Do they pump themselves up by making you look smaller? Do they exaggerate their own achievements and downplay the contributions of others? Do they shine in their own glory stories? All these are indicators that you are dealing with an ego-driven individual. It is quite easy to manage such types: all you need to do is feed their ego.

Pay attention to other tell-tale signs, such as attributes of status and power: fancy offices and lavishly furnished meeting rooms with huge meeting tables, show-off cars, expensive jewelry and accessories. Be on the lookout for other sources of power, specifically referent power (who are they associated with, with whom do they mingle, which club they belong to, and so on), and expertise power (titles, diplomas displayed on the walls).

The choice of career itself reveals the preferences in terms of lifestyle, professional tastes and interests, mental capabilities, and key competencies of a given person. We are what we do. Personality is shaped in equal part by heredity as by the socio-economic environment that we function in.

Lastly, your profiling stack should include the identification of the communication style of your negotiation partner. Is the message they convey explicitly transferred, or do you have to *read the air* to uncover the implicit meaning? Often, this is culturally embedded. Furthermore, is there evidence of a preference for a rational argument (I think, in my opinion, according to the data) or rather to emotion (I feel that, I sense, my intuition tells me). Search for any linguistic routines, jargon, or slang expressions indicative of educational, professional, and social status.

A thorough profiling is well worth the effort. You will collect a goldmine of information on your negotiation partner. This will allow you to structure your offer in a manner that is consistent with their inner identity system, thus increasing the chances of it being accepted with less of a struggle.

Key takeaways:
1. Work the man, not the case.
2. Profile your negotiation partner (identify their negotiation type, decision-making pattern, and reaction to stress).
3. Perform their personality assessment.
4. Check the accuracy of your perception and profiling results.
5. Pay attention to attributes of power, status, and ego.
6. Adapt your communication style to theirs (rational versus emotional).

Chapter 8: Further Reading

For an interdisciplinary outlook on which elements to pay attention to when you profile your negotiation partner, I suggest the following:

1. **Abraham H. Maslow,** *Motivation and Personality*
   Maslow introduced the famous concept of the Hierarchy of Needs (referred to as "Maslow's Pyramid"), which sheds light on the factors that drive human behavior. According to him, there is a continuum of elements that stimulate behavior. More specifically, there are five levels of needs: physiological, safety, belonging, esteem, and self-actualization. The main assumptions are that the lower-level needs have to be satisfied before passing on to the higher levels. Once a given need is fulfilled, it loses its power to motivate. At any given moment, multiple motivations can impact behaviors.
   🤝 **Tip for negotiators:** You need to understand how your offer will add value to your negotiation partner (not necessarily only in monetary terms). In order to do so, you must identify their prevalent needs.

2. **Kerrie Fleming,** *The Leader's Guide to Emotional Agility. How to Use Soft Skills to Get Hard Results*
   Emotional intelligence is the ability to recognize how your own feelings affect the person you are dealing with. It also means being aware of the emotions of others in order to manage them better. This book will help you understand yourself first, so that you can then profile your negotiation partner in a more conscious and bias-free manner.
   🤝 **Tip for negotiators:** An emotionally attuned negotiator picks up on the signals sent by their counterpart and can adjust their behavior accordingly. To reach executable agreements, you need to combine the soft skills with hard skills.

3. **Greg Williams, Pat Iyer,** *Body Language Secrets to Win More Negotiations. How to Read Any Opponent and Get What You Want*
   Another undercover element of profiling is reading body language. Body language is one of the types of communication (nonverbal)

that consists of: face and lips expressions, eye contact, use of gestures, movement of hands and feet, use of space, posture, and distance between people. The most important thing to take note of is that nonverbal communication is not static, but rather a dynamic process. Therefore, you will best observe the change in body language that follows after an emotional trigger is introduced.

Tip for negotiators: Watch out for the tell-tale signs that the body of your negotiator partner sends to you. Attention: if there is a discrepancy between the verbal and nonverbal message, trust the latter. The mouth can lie, the body does not.

CHAPTER 9

Choose the Right Strategy

THE Art of War, the iconic military treatise, begins with the description of the concept of *Ji*. It means plotting, planning, predicting, and analyzing—the ensemble of the steps that form the strategy of military action. Negotiation is not a war, but sometimes it may feel like it is. The two elements that govern any negotiation are task (the negotiation objective) and the relationship between the parties. These two factors are reflected either in the degree of assertiveness or the degree of cooperation. Task-oriented people will focus less on the relationship and the needs of the other party and will direct their energy toward reaching their objective. Consequently, their level of assertiveness will be higher. Relationship-oriented partners tend to be more cooperative. The task (T) and relationship (R) need to be considered before waging a negotiation. This is achieved by applying the appropriate negotiation strategy. You can choose between competition, compromise, avoidance, accommodation, and collaboration (win–win).

Competition is referred to as the *power struggle*, *law of the jungle*, or the *win–lose* approach. In French, it is called *rapport de force*, a definition that shows how power-oriented this strategy is. Competing involves a whole array of verbal, nonverbal, and para-verbal communication tactics aimed at making the other party comply with our demands. It is often characterized by aggressive or insulting behaviors, making the other party feel uncomfortable or weak, stating demands instead of investigating mutual interests, reluctance to making concessions, and trying to have our needs met at all costs. This approach seldom leads to sustainable agreements that bridge the task (negotiation objective) and relationship aspect. The main focus here is reaching your own objective (it's my way or the highway). This strategy is recommended in one-off transactions, for example, the sale of a used good where the buyer and seller both just want to strike the best deal and have no regard for future business.

Compromise is one of the easiest and fastest means of distribution of a limited resource. This strategy does not require too much time or creative effort on the part of the negotiating partners. In contrast to competition, a compromise does not mean that the winner takes it all. Ironically, it is another win–lose or lose–win approach to negotiation. In the course of mutual concessions, both parties gain and both lose something. As a visualization tool, compromise is often represented as an orange cut in two, of which one half goes to each party. The urban negotiation tale of two sisters quarreling over who will get the orange ends in their splitting the fruit in half. This is a fair and quick fix, but it is hardly the best one because it does not maximize the benefits flowing from the resource. After they split the fruit, it turned out that they wanted to use it for different aims (one for making juice and the other for the peel to add flavor to a cake).

Avoidance is considered a lose–lose strategy. It is mediocre both in the level of cooperation between the parties and in the level of individual assertiveness. This might be a good strategy if you want to wait things out, let emotions cool down, or prolong the process (during which you may occupy yourself with information gathering). The risk with avoidance is that the other party may perceive it as a lack of interest and priority on your part. This may adversely affect the relationship part. At the task level, obviously, things are at a standstill, which may make you look like a weak, reactive negotiator.

Accommodation, also referred to as yielding or lose–win, is an approach that places the relationship first. The level of cooperation is high, but assertiveness takes a hit. Often, this is the behavioral pattern exercised in families or between romantic partners. A business negotiation involves two parties with different needs trying to reach a mutually accepted agreement. As such, it is a two-sided process of persuading and convincing. Noteworthy, the key to long-lasting solutions is shaping the dynamic in such a way as to satisfy your own needs and to steer the other party toward compliance without detriment to either side's wants, needs, and negotiation goal. If you find that you have to continuously yield to your partner's needs, you will find yourself feeling emotionally abused. This will inevitably have a negative impact on the task constituent as well as the willingness to execute the terms of the agreement, provided one is reached.

Collaboration is associated with the theory of principled negotiation, which was developed by two Harvard professors Roger Fisher and William Ury in the 1980s. The theory has been transformed into a methodology—the systematic approach to negotiation. It has become synonymous with the more popular phrase *win–win*—originally taken from game theory. Contrary to positional bargaining, which, as the name itself suggests, means locking oneself in a fixed position, principled negotiation leads to an agreement that should be efficient in the distribution of the resource(s), fair to both sides, and reinforcing the relationship between them. This approach involves, among others, finding arrangements by identifying the interests behind the positions and determining which needs are fixed and which are flexible for negotiators, and then finding creative options to bridge those needs. On the scale between task and relationship, this is the strategy that balances both these elements.

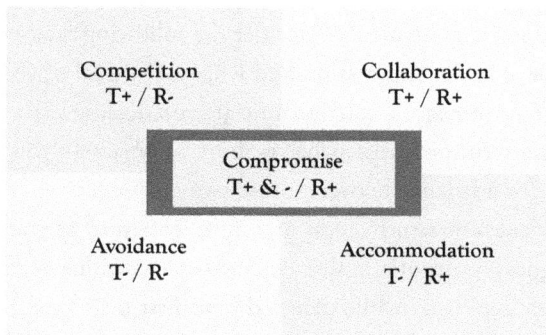

Competition
T+ / R-

Collaboration
T+ / R+

Compromise
T+ & -/ R+

Avoidance
T- / R-

Accommodation
T- / R+

Figure 9.9 Negotiation strategies—task and relationship

There is no law that says you need to limit yourself to using only one strategy. A negotiation is like trying to get from point A to B. You know where you want to end up, but you might encounter adventures on your way. You need to be flexible and adapt to the situational context and the behavior of your negotiation partner. You may consider applying what I call the hybrid approach. It is a mix of the different strategies. You can start with a forceful approach, break your counterpart in, and test their pain threshold. Plant the seeds in their mind of what your goal is, aim big. Then back off from the task, do not pressure, do not insist. Give it space and time, avoid for a moment. Meanwhile, you may accommodate by tending more to the relationship. Strengthen the bond with your negotiation partner. You might make a few concessions by trading the things that have little importance to you or even compromise in this phase. Then, depending on the nature of the transaction, either compete or collaborate with full speed ahead.

The choice of negotiation strategy also depends on the individual inclinations of the parties and the level of faith they have in each other. The Prisoner's Dilemma uncovers the paradox that two negotiators driven solely by suspicion and self-interest do not produce the best outcomes for either of them.

An expert negotiator has the ability to fulfill several roles and draw from a wide variety of skills. The choice of negotiation strategy governs success and therefore must be understood in the planning and execution of the negotiation. This will require you to be a master strategist with a global, long-term vision. When choosing the best approach, you need to perform a strategic assessment. Consider the following factors: what you want to achieve in the negotiation and what is the goal of your counterpart, which type of negotiation dynamic are you dealing with, what is the short- or long-term potential, what is more important—the task or the relationship (or a balance between those two elements), what is the level of cooperativeness or assertiveness of your negotiation partner, as well as their willingness to negotiate. Remember that victorious negotiators win first and then negotiate, while defeated ones first negotiate and then try to win.

Key takeaways:
1. Balance the task and relationship.
2. Pay attention to the level of assertiveness or cooperation of your negotiation partner.
3. Depending on that level, adopt the appropriate strategy.
4. Choose competition for one-off transactions.
5. Never compromise to save the relationship.
6. Use the hybrid approach (a mix of all five strategies) for different phases of the negotiation.

Chapter 9: Further Reading

Strategic preparation combined with self-empowerment are a bulletproof mix for achieving success in negotiations. For a broader idea on how to choose the right strategy, take a look at the following:

1. **Sun Tzu, *The Art of War***

   The ancient Chinese military treatise dating back to the 5th century BC, which provides an ageless framework for strategic preparation, applicable to business as much as warfare. Master Sun makes the famous statement that "Victorious warriors win first and then go to war, while defeated warriors go to war first and then seek to win" (Page 10). The treaty guides the reader through the six steps of strategic approach: Tao (moral standing), Tien (timing), Di (terrain, resources), Jiang (leadership), Fa (management), and Ji (planning).

   🤝 **Tip for negotiators:** Follow this ancient wisdom and let it lead you to success in your negotiations.

2. **Chin-Ning Chu, *The Art of War for Women: It's About the Art, Not the War***

   True to the old Chinese saying: "Shang chang ru zhan chang" (the marketplace is a battlefield), this book provides a blueprint for success for women leaders. It builds on the concepts of the famous military treaty (the six steps of strategic approach constitute its framework), and further adopts it to modern business practice and bridges strategic execution with self-empowerment. It provides precious insights about the mistakes that female professionals make that hinder their career development.

   Food for thought: "The woman from Mars is a nitpicker. Her need for perfection makes her intolerant of everything. She'll never be CEO" (Page 135).

   🤝 **Tip for negotiators:** "Successful women worldwide have one thing in common: They don't see the glass ceiling" (Page 75). Remember that victory is in your mind first.

3. **Laurence Bergreen, *Casanova. The World of a Seductive Genius***

"Love and war are the same thing, and stratagems and policy are as allowable in the one as in the other" (Miguel de Cervantes). Many have heard about Casanova, most see him as the world's most skilled seducer, few know that he was a great strategist, both in the alcove and beyond. The question is, what made him so successful. If there was only one word to describe Casanova, it would be perseverance. Once he set his mind (and heart) on a target, he would pursue that target until he obtained it. Proof: Casanova spent several years in prison having been sentenced there for his entanglement in political affairs. He literally dug himself out of the dungeons and escaped. His success with the opposite sex was largely due to a combination of perseverance and choosing the right strategy to woo his object of desire.

Tip for negotiators: Choose your target, keep your eye on the prize, and never give up your pursuit.

CHAPTER 10

How to Impact Behavior: The Feel–Think–Act Trio

ONE of the differentiating traits of high-impact leaders and business professionals is a strong focus on goal achievement. A proactive approach and task orientation allow them to not only get the job done, but also excel over competition. Perhaps, you see a reflection of yourself in this description and contentedly think that you tick the boxes for negotiation success. Please note that I used the words "leaders and business professionals," and not negotiators. Perhaps you are slightly confused now. While it is recommended that you should display a proactive attitude in a negotiation, drive the process and keep your eyes on the prize, a one-sided focus on action alone will not translate into success.

A negotiation consists of three types of behaviors: influencing, convincing, and persuading. To influence means to have an effect on the behavior of someone. To convince primarily means to make someone believe in something. To persuade is to induce someone to do something through argumentative reasoning. A negotiation is an interaction between two parties with different interests who try to reach an agreement that bridges those interests, and thus satisfies the individual motives of each party. The role of a negotiator is to change the attitude of the other party toward the interests that we are trying to fulfill. According to cognitive behavioral therapy (CBT), an attitude is a cocktail of cognitive (thoughts), affective (feelings), and behavioral (actions) elements. In order to change the attitude of your negotiation partner, you need to address all three elements. The secret of success lies in the sequence of how this is done.

Some negotiators focus all their energy on attempting to change the behavior of the other party. In other words, they resort to the art of influence. It is noteworthy that profession creates trained patterns of professional conduct, which then has a direct reflection in the adopted negotiation approach. Salespeople or project managers usually tend to start with action orientation. Lawyers direct their attention to argument preparation; they resort to the tools of oratory persuasion. Meanwhile, the change in behavioral pattern is the last instance. In order to impact how a person will act, it is necessary to first modify how they feel and think.

The brain is built in such a way that when an external trigger enters, it first reaches the amygdala, which is a cluster of neurons located in the brain's medial temporal lobe that forms part of the limbic system. The amygdala plays a key role in processing emotions. In a very simplified illustration, once the trigger passes the amygdala, it reaches the neocortex, which is a region responsible for, among others, cognition, perception, and logical reasoning. Contrary to what we would like to think, biology suggests that humans are primarily emotional beings. Studies in psychology, decision-making, and behavioral economics confirm the assumption that there are two systems—System 1 is responsible for the quick associations and mental shortcuts, it operates on the basis of feelings. System 2 is the more complex representative of logic and reasoning. The conclusion is clear: we first feel, then we think. In more elaborate terms, we rationalize the reasons to justify the emotional decisions we had already made.

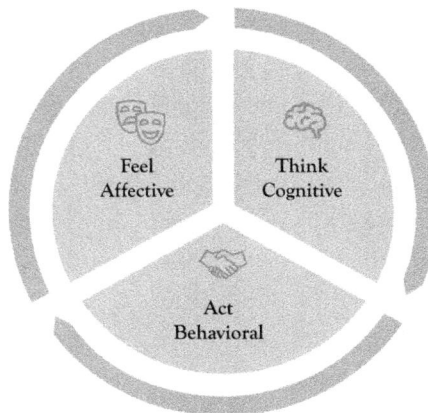

Figure 10.10 The feel–think–act trio[6]

---

[6] The ACB model was adapted from Slocum, J.W., and D. Hellriegel. 2011. Principles of Organizational Behavior. South-Western Cengage Learning.

A skilled negotiator will use this knowledge to their advantage. The next time you want to change the behavior of your negotiation partner, apply the feel–think–act approach. Start with inflicting certain emotions. This can be done in multiple ways. The way you welcome someone, how you design the meeting space, the small courtesies (or lack thereof) that you extend their way, what you say, and how you and your surrounding look will all create certain emotions. For example, many executives shared with me that such a simple act as not being offered coffee by the counterpart at the beginning of a negotiation has emotionally derailed them. They perceived the lack of this beverage, traditionally associated with a welcome gesture, as a symbol of inequality of power and *showing them their inferiority*. Small symbolic rituals can have a profound effect.

The first few minutes after the external trigger enters the brain are critical, because the person is emotionally destabilized and therefore exposed. In order for the interaction to be based on reason, you should stabilize your negotiation partner (and yourself). You can use the good-old tactic of small talk. It seems innocent enough to talk about trivial matters; however, if conducted properly, it is an excellent opportunity to gather information about your negotiation partner and to test the accuracy of your own perceptions. It is also the phase during which you tend to the relationship part of the negotiation equation. In some cultures, small talk is an indispensable element of the negotiation mating game, and failure to engage in it may dampen the chances of an agreement being reached. Once you have caused certain emotions, you can then lead your partner to a certain cognitive path that you have pre-paved for them. The play on emotions is a tool used for evoking thoughts and certain automatic reactions. When you inflict emotions, you should, therefore, be crystal clear about where that path will lead to.

The last step is the behavioral change you want to happen. It is a sign of moral standing and a strong moral backbone if one *walks the talk*, in other words, if the behavior is consistent with the words one utters. People tend to have strong reactions toward a phenomenon that is referred to as cognitive dissonance. This term refers to a situation that involves conflicting emotions, values, and behaviors. This results in a feeling of mental discomfort, which leads to an alteration in behavior to reduce the discomfort and restore balance. You can create cognitive dissonance to impact the behavior of your negotiation partner. If you are making a big demand, think of a smaller one that is likely to be accepted, because it is aligned with their system of beliefs or values. Have them commit to this minor demand and then present the bigger one as a natural consequence. A rejection would cause loss of face due to cognitive inconsistency.

Work on the natural tendency of people to rationalize their decisions based on the affective element. In order for people to accept your negotiation proposal, they need to feel that they were involved in the process. For example, conscious mental (rational) acceptance of certain arrangements will only be possible if they are consistent with the person's inner convictions. The latter are closely related to feelings. Consequently, do not offer ready solutions. Resist the urge to focus solely on the act you want to happen. Make your partner *feel like* they contributed, they will find reasons to rationalize the agreement on their own. "Remember that he that complies against his will, is of his opinion still" (S. Butler).

Key takeaways:
1. In order to change how your negotiation partner will act, modify how they feel and think first.
2. Apply the feel–think–act approach.
3. Inflict certain emotions (in yourself and your negotiation partner) that will support your negotiation objective.
4. Stabilize your negotiation partner (and yourself) with small talk.
5. Create cognitive dissonance to impact the behavior of your negotiation partner.
6. Do not offer ready solutions. Make your partner *feel like* they contributed to the process.

Chapter 10: Further Reading

The following books will help you uncover how to channel the potential of your mind to influence the behavior of yourself and your negotiation partner:

1. **Amy Cuddy, *Presence. Bringing Your Boldest Self to Your Biggest Challenges***
   We all know that the mind governs the body, but what if we reverse this dynamic—does the body have an impact on our mind, too?

This is one of the many fascinating questions that Cuddy addresses in her book. She proves that altering the position of our body, by assuming certain *power postures*, such as the famous Wonder Woman pose, can reduce the level of cortisol (the stress hormone), and increase the level of testosterone. This translates into an enhanced sense of self-control, empowerment, and less aversion to risk-taking. This might well be one of the easiest techniques of elevating your power in the negotiation.

Tip for negotiators: Strike a (power) pose before your next negotiation.

2. **Robert Greene, *Mastery***

Mastery is "the feeling that we have a greater command of reality, other people, and ourselves" (Page 3). It is the emotional quality that differentiates those who master certain skills from those who simply perform them. In this insightful book, the author takes us through the stages of achieving mastery. The effort is well worth it. Greene proves that our feelings and thoughts create our mental landscape, which then shapes the patterns of what ultimately happens to us. In other words, the first step toward external wins is always an inward journey.

Tip for negotiators: Mastery is dependent on the intensity of your focus (Page 190). Shape the feel–think–act trio to fit your desired negotiation outcome.

3. **Scott Adams, *Loserthink. How Untrained Brains are Ruining the World.***

Loserthink is a concept that depicts using the brain in unproductive ways. Sadly, this is the case more often than one would like to admit. The result is that much intellectual effort and mental energy goes to waste. The evidence is ever-present: many business meetings lose focus, teams fall into the trap of groupthink, choices are made based on information bias, negotiations end in irrelevant debates. Adams attempts to free the reader from certain mental constraints by guiding toward a more effective cognitive effort. He uncovers how psychologists, artists, historians, engineers, leaders, scientists, entrepreneurs, and economists think.

Tip for negotiators: Have you built your own mental prison? If so, break out of it and start thinking like an effective negotiator.

CHAPTER 11

On Listening: The Ego Whisperer

THE success of a negotiation depends on your ability to manage yourself, your own emotions, and your ego. We are all our own most important persona. The selfie culture grants legitimacy to self-concentration and gives it a public arena to thrive in. The most difficult part may be to direct the spotlight from yourself and to your negotiation partner, to listen to their reasoning and only then steer the negotiation toward the technical details. The feeling of being heard and understood can bring down defenses better than the most elaborate tactic. In sales and customer service trainings, a lot of time is spent on effective listening skills, not just on making sales pitches.

If we were to imagine the listening process on a scale from 0 to 100, typically, we stop listening to the other person at about 20 percent. We hear what they are saying (in the physical sense of registering the sound), we can even give off the impression that we are attentive by nodding our head and displaying other affirmative gestures, by maintaining eye contact, and by applying the necessary para-verbals. However, the truth is that we are not really listening, and we are by far the great pretenders. Most of the executives and students I work with admitted that they can pretend to be listening, and that they can also sense when the other party is faking it.

Listening is a critical skill because it allows you to unblock your partner's resistance to your offer, helps you create a bond, and equips you with precious information on how to reach the objectives of the negotiation. Here are the most common mistakes and some practical suggestions on how to enrich your personal listening inventory.[7]

---

[7] Adapted from Obliger, D. 2018. Life or Death Listening. A Hostage Negotiator's How-to Guide to Mastering the Essential Communication Skill. USA: Amazon Kindle Direct Publishing.

Listening inventory	Tips for effective listening
Do you listen to hear the words, or do you listen to understand the meaning?	The next time you listen to someone, do not concentrate on the words (listening is not the ability to repeat back, word-for-word what was said), but rather try to get to the core of the story and what the speaker is trying to convey. Example: from what I hear, it seems that keeping control of your company is something very important for you.
Do you cut-in or finish sentences for the speaker?	Refrain from the urge to interrupt. There is always new information to be discovered. No, you do not know it all, nobody does. You also cannot predict the future. By finishing someone's sentences for them, you deceive yourself that you can. If you have not asked and listened, you do not know.
Do you overtake the other's story?	Typically confused with creating a bond. Overtaking refers to the situation when the other party shares an experience and you immediately respond by sharing your own similar experience. To you, it seems like you are bonding by showing that you can relate to their story. To them, you are competing, or alternatively, making the conversation about you. Listen to their story patiently, yours can wait.
Are you distracted while the other person is speaking?	Many executives ask me how to keep focus when the other party is *extremely boring*. Approach the situation as a technical exercise, give your brain a task to fulfill, for example, profiling of the person. To complete that mission, you will need to concentrate on the speaker in order to collect the necessary data. The boredom aspect will soon be forgotten. If you are distracted in the negotiation, you might need to postpone it (if possible) until you sort out the source of your mental diversion. Otherwise, you risk not paying attention to the small details that often jeopardize the deal. If postponing is not an option, try to mentally leave the source of your distraction outside the negotiation room.
Do you give appropriate encouragers?	Apply encouragers when you listen to the other party—the nonverbal gestures and vocal para-verbals that invite them to proceed with their message. It is critical that the encouragers are combined with intentional listening; otherwise, the effect lacks authenticity and will create more harm than good.
Are you like an interrogator?	Pose open questions that steer the exchange toward your desired outcome. Minimize the number of questions; by limiting their number, you will be forced to select only the most important ones. Weave in summaries or paraphrases of what you heard to disrupt the question-answer interrogation vibe.

Do you listen only long enough to decide how you will counter?	Listen for new information, a fresh outlook, to discover something that will allow you to adapt to the negotiation. If you cut the listening process short, you risk a premature response based on incomplete information that will be detrimental to your position in the negotiation.
How often do you need to ask others to repeat themselves?	If this is done frequently, it is a clear sign to the other party that you have not been paying attention. For most of us, this is equivalent to lack of respect that can harm the relationship aspect of the negotiation. If you have to ask the counterpart to repeat themselves, let it be known that what they have to say is important for you, and that you want to make sure you did not miss anything. Do not do this often.

Listening is a delicate art of self- and ego-management. The most difficult part for the ego to accept is that when it comes to listening, it is not about you. In the process, be ready to uncover truths that may be unpleasant, even then refrain from judging, offering unsolicited advice, or expressing your opinions from a patronizing standpoint. Develop a mindset of unconditional positive regard. Positivity attracts positive people, behaviors, and events. Never assume the negative, at the minimum, keep a neutral stance. Listen, do not problem-solve. Listening means only doing two things at once: concentrating on the speaker and showing understanding (not equivalent to agreeing).

To become a master listener, never miss a listening opportunity. Practice your skill every day, at work, at home, with your friends. You will reap the benefits in your next negotiation. If you are too busy to listen, you are too busy and will pay the price later in the form of money left on the table and less-than-desirable negotiation outcomes.

Listening can be mentally and emotionally straining, especially because we are so used to talking. Habitual activities take up less energy than new patterns of behavior. Get a daily dose of silence that will allow you to detox auditorily from the information overflow that is distracting your mind and making it difficult to grasp the hidden messages in all those exchanges that you engage in. Make a pact with yourself and your ego to speak only if it improves upon the silence.

Key takeaways:
1. Direct the spotlight from yourself to your negotiation partner, listen to their reasoning, then steer the negotiation toward the technical details.
2. Listen for the meaning, not the words.
3. Do not cut-in, finish sentences for the speaker, or overtake their story.
4. Stay focused so that the speaker does not have to repeat themselves.
5. Give appropriate encouragers.
6. Do not fire questions like an interrogator.
7. Listen until the end and only then respond.

Chapter 11: Further Reading

In order to unlock your listening potential, it is beneficial to first understand the basics of rhetoric. After all, you need to know what exactly you are listening *for*.

1. **Marcus Tullius Cicero, *How to Win an Argument. An Ancient Guide to the Art of Persuasion* (selected, edited, and translated by James M. May)**

   The ancient guide to the art of rhetoric. Oratory eloquence encompasses much more than solely the application of persuasive arguments. The ideal orator should possess an array of other skills, such as a vast knowledge of a given topic combined with the study of human nature, enriched by the ability to listen to the arguments of the other party, and supported by diligent practical application of the findings. This is consistent with the synergistic approach to negotiation—a master negotiator should know the topic (the task at hand), but must also be able to appeal to the human factor.

   Tip for negotiators: Tailor the approach to the individual by focusing all your attention on listening to both the tactical details and the person.

2. **Jay Heinrichs, *Thank You for Arguing. What Cicero, Shakespeare and the Simpsons Can Teach Us About the Art of Persuasion***

   This book, as many others, approaches the topic of persuasion from the angle of one-sided focus, for example: "make them listen"

(Chapter 6). While the ideas are good, the practical approach could benefit from a technical twist. The classic design of a persuasive argument is built around the following three elements: reason (ethos), logic (logos), and passion (pathos). The aim of these qualities is to enhance the audience's receptiveness, attentiveness, and favorable disposition toward your proposal. What if the dynamic was shifted?

Tip for negotiators: Structure your arguments in accordance with these oratory rules, but also listen to seek out these elements in your negotiation partners' rhetoric. This will allow you to identify the logic and emotions behind their reasoning. You can then target your offer accordingly and minimize the risk of it falling on deaf ears.

3. **Dale Carnegie, *How to Win Friends and Influence People***
A timeless book packed with practical insights on how to increase your acceptance in social circumstances and in business. Socializing and negotiations have something in common: they often start with small talk. It is a means of breaking the ice, addressing the relationship (and not only the task), and emotionally stabilizing yourself and the other party before moving on to the objective of the meeting. The thought of engaging in small talk makes some of us cringe. If you ever wondered what makes a good conversationalist, you might be relieved: it is the ability to listen intently.

Tip for negotiators: If you want to influence people, you will need to listen to them first.

CHAPTER 12

Two-Dimensional Listening

NEGOTIATION is commonly associated with oratory excellence, argumentative prowess, and virtuosity of the tools of verbal communication. That is only part of the skillset of a master negotiator. The best negotiators are not those who talk the most, but those who listen more than they speak. Despite what it may seem on the surface, silence is not an exercise in procrastination. Listening is, in fact, a sophisticated, two-dimensional process.

On the external level, it involves what is referred to as *reading the air* or *reading between the words*, understanding the real message hidden behind the words. This requires close attention to the choice and types of words used, their emotional or rational charge, the perception of reality that the speaker unveils, and the manner in which the message is conveyed (para-verbal communication). All these elements allow for profiling of your negotiation partner—their emotional state, personality type, social status, self-evaluation, education level, intercultural sensitivity, and so on. Decoding the real meaning of the message will help you understand your negotiation partner, a critical foundation for further interaction with them.

On the internal level, the process of listening is even more complex, as it calls for switching off the self-centered mode. This is becoming an increasingly difficult task for the representatives of the selfie generation. Next time you negotiate with someone, and it is their turn to speak, stop yourself for a moment to analyze what your mind is doing. You will start by listening, but then you will notice your ears losing focus. What will inevitably be happening are several things: you may stop listening because you think you know what will be said, you might be making conscious or unconscious judgments about the other person, it is highly likely you are planning what you will say, and preparing your counter-arguments. Look at all the things that are happening simultaneously and competing for your attention. No wonder the conscious act of directed listening is so difficult!

I understood this on one of my business trips to Italy. I cannot speak Italian, but I can comprehend most of what is said. During this particular mission, I was assisting my business mentor in a mediation session in family court. The case involved the division of the heritage between several heirs, and the emotions were high for all those involved. My role was to listen in and then prepare a debriefing of what I saw and heard. Due to my linguistic limitations, I was literally the silent observer. At first, it felt a bit constraining not to be able to join the exchange. Nonetheless, it was a welcome change for me to be in a position where I did not need to prepare a riposte, impress anyone, or win the other party over by arguments. Liberated from this pressure, I was astonished to see how my focus switched to limitless listening. I took everything in—the verbal supported by the extensive nonverbal, the hidden messages that were floating through the air, the ego interplays, and the interpersonal dynamic. It was one of the most mind-, eye-, and ear-opening experiences in my career. It made me realize how little people who are seemingly involved in a discussion truly listen to each other. They mostly communicate with themselves. From the perspective of a nonparticipant, the effect is quite entertaining, but not in a good way.

Try to find that place in your mind in your next negotiation. You will need to train yourself to take control over the temptation to immediately verbalize your thoughts. Instead, control and direct the flow of mental energy into listening rather than speaking. It will help direct your focus to the unspoken needs of the other party, which will make it much easier to tailor your offer, strategy, and approach accordingly. Remember, speech is silver, but silence is golden.

Key takeaways:
1. Listen more than you speak.
2. Listen to understand the real message hidden behind the words.
3. Listen to understand your negotiation partner.
4. Resist the temptation to immediately verbalize your thoughts.
5. Control and direct the flow of mental energy into listening rather than speaking.
6. Focus on the un-verbalized needs of the other party.

Chapter 12: Further Reading

The following package will provide more details on the topic of listening:

1. **Dan Oblinger, *The 28 Laws of Listening. Best Practices for the Master Listener***

   As the title suggests, the book is a condensed compilation of the 28 best practices for a master listener. Drawing from his practice as a hostage negotiator, the author leads the reader through the methods and techniques of active listening.

   My personal favorite: Give unconditional positive regard (the 25th law).

   🤝 **Tip for negotiators:** Get in the habit of listening more than you speak.

2. **Dan Obliger, *Life or Death Listening. A Hostage Negotiator's How-to Guide to Mastering the Essential Communication Skill***

   An extinction alert to the dying art of listening caused by the information overflow and cacophony of the digitalization that competes for our attention. The author shows that listening is not a function of the ears alone, but rather of the mind and soul. It is the foundation of human communication and long-lasting relationships, both personal and professional.

   🤝 **Tip for negotiators:** Listen as if your life depended on it.

3. **William Ury, *Getting Past No. Negotiating with Difficult People***

   Negotiators are constantly seeking ways to cut down on their costs and maximize the gains. Ury suggests that "Listening to someone may be the cheapest concession you can make" (Page 37). He invites the reader to step out of the cycle and monologues and become a pioneer in the art of listening. You will surely uncover new information and, who knows, maybe you will even become a trend-setter. Does this not sound tempting?

   🤝 **Tip for negotiators:** Disarm your counterpart by granting them the courtesy of listening.

CHAPTER 13

On Creating a Bond: Tell Me a Story

ONE of the business professionals whom I trained shared with me the story of an enriching experience that she had while coaching a young professional from the Middle East. He was doing an apprenticeship to take over his family business imperium. Her role was to prepare him strategically, enhance his leadership skills, and prepare him for the multi-stakeholder negotiations he would soon be involved in. Their professional journey lasted several years during which the role of mentor and student intertwined. To describe their beginnings as rocky would be a euphemism. There was literally a world of differences between them in terms of nationality, family traditions and upbringing, culture, customs, religion, gender and related hierarchical roles, as well as values and beliefs. They both have strong personalities and rigid viewpoints on certain topics that are important for them. Despite the divergences, they managed to find a common ground and create a bond that allowed them to survive the clash of the titans and fulfill the objectives of their assignment. This experience shows that a bond between the parties is a critical success factor for long-lasting business relationships. In order to build it, you will need to follow several phases. It all starts with telling a story.

| Phase 1: Story | Phase 2: Emotions | Phase 3: Perception | Phase 4: Empathy | Phase 5: Trust | Phase 6: Bond |

Figure 13.11 Listening as a process

Having been educated and having spent most of her professional life in a task-oriented business culture, her approach to getting things done was primarily focused on the assignment itself. Before taking on this assignment, she thought that the relation part was an aftermath. His view was the opposite; before the task came the relationship part of the business transaction. She was surprised when he used to ask: "Tell me a story" at the beginning of most of their sessions. At first, she did not know what story to tell, she searched in her mind for a topic related to the task they had planned for the day trying to think of something business savvy to say. This was not what he was looking for. He wanted her own story. It could be anything: an image she saw driving between my meetings, a song she heard that inspired her, a comment or remark that caught her attention. What was important was that she could convey to him the emotion evoked by that trigger. It was his way of understanding her reality, the way she made sense of the world, how she felt on a given day, what was her mood and her current emotional inventory. That perceptual collage would inevitably define the dynamic of their meeting on a given day. This is a valuable lesson for negotiations. Very often, a proposal will fall on deaf ears if your partner is not in a receptive mood. It is all about the right timing.

The ability to perceive and understand the world through the lens of your partner and relate to their feelings is what we refer to as empathy. Please note that it is not equivalent to agreeing; therefore, it does not have any adverse effect on the task you want to achieve. In negotiations, this can be used as a powerful tool of deblocking the other party and making them less defensive and thus more receptive to your proposal. This creates the foundation for them to trust you. Noteworthy, trust is seen as the condition for any business (and personal) relationship with long-term potential. Think of trust as a positive reserve that you should invest in, just like you put money in your savings account for a rainy day. The trick is to have a positive account balance that can offset any obstacles that you will inevitably face on the path to reaching an agreement. An arrangement based on mutual understanding and bonding is unbreakable. Sometimes, it can be life-changing, as in the case of the Prisoner's Dilemma. If both parties trust each other and have faith that their individual interests will not take priority, then they can each benefit from a lower sentence and clean conscience.

Many negotiators face the same challenges that the business professional initially did when asked to tell her story. We are our own most severe critics. The participants in my negotiation trainings struggle with telling a story. They fear how others will perceive them and how they will be judged, even though they are in a safe training environment. The outcome is inevitably the same—the stories are either told in a timid way or with overdone poise meant to disguise inner insecurities. This immediately sends a signal of lack of conviction and takes away from their authority. Some have become so mechanic in their approach that it is difficult for them to be creative. This has a reflection in their negotiation style—often, these are the negotiators who find it difficult to think *outside the box* (a term they like to use but do not necessarily apply) and who tend to get stuck in their rigid positions. Such an attitude may lead to an impasse and ultimately jeopardize the chances of reaching an agreement.

Be proud of your story, own it, and present it with dignity in a self-empowered manner. Do not be afraid to show your human side. Empathy is not a sign of weakness. It is the only way to build and bond. Even in tough negotiations or when faced with the Prisoner's Dilemma, an agreement based on mutual understanding and bonding is unbreakable. Remember that business is usually personal.

Key takeaways:
1. Create a bond between yourself and your negotiation partner.
2. Approach listening as a process (story-> emotions-> perception -> empathy -> trust -> bond).
3. Carefully choose the right time for your proposal.
4. Use empathy to deblock the other party and make them less defensive.
5. Invest in a trust reserve, it will reap future benefits.
6. Let your own story empower you.

Chapter 13: Further Reading

With the passing of time, people will forget what you said and which exact words you used, but they will never forget how you made them feel. A good story will do just that; it will stay engraved in the heart and mind. Here are the recommended choices of enlightening stories that will help you discover simple truths for your negotiations:

1. **Spencer Johnson, *Who Moved My Cheese? An A-mazing Way to Deal with Change in Your Work and in Your Life***
   Advertised as one of the most successful business books of all times, this booklet lives up to its reputation. A parable of two mice and two

men who are in a maze where they search for and consume cheese. The cheese is a metaphor for success and achievement. The quest for it is much like navigating the labyrinth of life. It will require drive, mental stamina, the ability to deal with change, problem-solving skills, and team spirit. One day, the cheese is taken away, and that is when the characters are put to the test. I leave you to discover who manages to overcome this challenge better.

Tip for negotiators: Never take anything for granted in a negotiation (or beyond), continuously improve on your options.

2. **Edith Eger, *The Choice. Even in Hell Hope Can Flower***

A memoir of the survivor of Holocaust, *the ballerina of Auschwitz*, a deeply moving, powerful, and disturbing study of human nature. This book will put into perspective the meaning of what is important in life and what a *life-or-death negotiation* really is.

Years after she is freed from Auschwitz, she manages to rebuild her life. Together with her husband, she plans to move to the United States where they will be war immigrants. On the eve of their departure, her husband is captivated in a raid for Jewish people. Eger finds herself having to negotiate with a guard to free her husband from prison. This is the ultimate life-or-death negotiation. The most powerful message that Eger conveys is that you can be victimized, but choose never to be a victim.

Tip for negotiators: You control how the events in your life affect you. Use that ability to succeed in your most difficult negotiations.

3. **Bob Burg, John David Mann, *The Go-Giver Influencer. A Little Story About a Most Persuasive Idea***

An eye-opening anecdote for the go-getters in business negotiations. A story of two negotiators whose fixation on their own goals prevents them from seeing the needs of the other party and how these interests can overlap. A refreshing approach to the topic of finding common ground in negotiation.

Tip for negotiators: Do not let yourself be driven by self-interest, give to get.

CHAPTER 14

Beyond Mars and Venus: Gender and Negotiations

THE aim of profiling is to gather information that will allow you to understand the individual characteristics of the person you will be dealing with, such as personality, intercultural exposure, life experiences and business acumen, which all have an impact on the negotiation process. One of the key differentiating factors and sources of diversity is gender; hence, it is helpful to know what the distinguishing characteristics of female and male negotiators are. This chapter is not a gender manifesto, but rather a compilation of certain behavioral patterns that may impact the negotiation power of both men and women. Although some may seem prevalent for one sex than the other, it is not meant to be taken as a stereotypical guide to feminine and masculine patterns of behavior. The topic merits a thorough analysis of the biological, historical, and societal role of both sexes, which lies outside the scope of this book.

One of the young executives whom I was preparing for an upcoming negotiation made an interesting remark when I asked her which strategy she will adopt. Her reply was, "I will negotiate like a man." The theory of negotiation enumerates compromise, competition, collaboration, avoidance, or accommodation as the available options, possibly a hybrid version of all of them. The existing research on negotiation does not include the negotiation approach "like a man." Nonetheless, I knew what she meant. I also understood what a male participant in one of the executive trainings had in mind when he said "it must have been a woman" in reference to a mock negotiation scenario with a difficult counterpart. Both were referring to caricatures of certain traits attributed to each gender.

Stereotypes are dangerous, mind-limiting, and, quite often, inaccurate. Each negotiator is different and cannot be classified based on gender alone. Nonetheless, stereotypes reflect a collective memory of certain predominant patterns of behavior of a specific group. Therefore, it is helpful to know what they are in order to rise above the limitations they carry. Furthermore, recognition of gender differences may allow negotiators of both sexes to maximize on their diversity in reaching better agreements. Collaboration usually bears sweeter fruit than a war of the sexes.

For biological reasons, the role of a woman is more linked to caretaking. Historically, upbringing and socialization often enforced and gave this role legitimacy. As a consequence, women have a tendency to be relationship-oriented and cooperative, whereas men give task achievement priority. Women might compromise or accommodate, while men would tend to compete more. Studies show that, on average, female negotiators are less prone to risk-taking. In communication, they like to get to the bottom of the matter, which is a strong advantage in identifying the interests behind the positions in a negotiation.

I have encountered female negotiators who either want to defy this role completely and imitate men, or those who are more or less comfortable with their femininity at the negotiation table. The feeling of comfort in one's own skin often comes with experience and seniority (sadly not always). The first group are women who tend to be overly aggressive, loud, domineering, and often arrogant. They emphasize the struggles they have been through, assert their rights (often with arguments related to gender), and sometimes intimidate the other party by recourse to various sources of power. It is worth pointing out that extremes are seldom a sign of self-empowerment and power, a statement that applies to male executives in the same manner.

The second type are women who try to bridge their femininity and professional conduct. I used the word *try* deliberately, because it is a considerable effort. The reality is such that women are still outnumbered by men in board rooms, business meetings, and at the negotiation table in many industries on a worldwide scale. Many of them suffer from the impostor syndrome, the feeling that they do not belong, or the disbelief that they really made it that far. The result is that they take up less space (in the physical and meta-physical sense), do not bring many demands to the table, either do not ask at all or ask for less than their male counterparts.

They also make more concessions than male negotiators would in order to save or not jeopardize the relationship. They often apologize for expressing their opinions and ask for permission to contribute to the negotiation, failing to realize that they are equal partners in the negotiation. Female negotiators should claim their status and role in the negotiation in a self-conscious, assertive, and graceful manner.

A reoccurring remark about male negotiators is that they tend to be more ego-sensitive and prone to getting on their high horse to prove their point or assert their status in a negotiation. In order to do so, they might emphasize their position, which may lead to a deadlock. In general, men have less difficulty with drawing a clear line between the task and the relationship. Provided their ego does not get in the way, they negotiate on the merits of the case. While rejection may bruise their ego and shake up their inner sense of self-worth, proposing lies in their DNA. Therefore, bringing more demands and raising the stakes come more naturally to them.

How can you use these insights to enrich your negotiations? Diversity often unveils its full potential in turbulent circumstances. When negotiations reach an impasse, it is helpful to switch the dynamic around a bit. This may mean changing the scenery, taking time off to cool the emotions, modifying the adopted strategy, or altering the team structure. In practical terms, this sometimes means adding more female or male representatives to the negotiation. This will inevitably lead to looking at things from a different perspective. As each sex has its unique strong sides, a fusion of masculine and feminine traits can lead to more rounded negotiation outcomes.

For all the negotiators, whether from Mars or Venus, do not allow gender stereotypes to lower your inner bargaining power. Subtle cues such as timidity, hesitation, fear, self-doubt, or lack of conviction radiate externally, bring your own negotiation status down and give a reason for the counterpart to attack you. Acknowledge diversity as a source of richness. Remember that power is an elusive concept; if you think you have it, then you do; if you think you do not, then you do not. This has nothing to do with gender, but everything to do with how you see yourself in the negotiation.

Key takeaways:
1. Let your gender traits be a source of strength rather than an impediment.
2. Understand the differences between female and male negotiation styles.
3. Do not defy the gender roles or try to artificially overcross them to mimic the other sex.
4. Avoid the impostor syndrome (the feeling you are not a legitimate player).
5. Claim your status and role in the negotiation in a self-conscious and assertive manner.
6. Do not allow gender stereotypes to limit your inner negotiation power.

Chapter 14: Further Reading

This chapter is not designed to be a feminist manifesto nor is it meant to add fuel to the gender movement. Its aim is rather to show that gender diversity, as any other form of diversity, is a source of richness for individuals and organizations. More importantly, it highlights certain shortcomings of humanity as a whole, for which gender often becomes a convenient scapegoat. The more we understand our unique differences, the more we can maximize the benefits flowing from working together. The following start-kit will help you understand what are the factors that impact the female and male negotiation styles:

1. **Simone de Beauvoir, *The Second Sex***

   An absolute classic for any reader, female or male, which lays out the evolution of a woman's condition and the societal factors that define her role. An interesting observation is the reciprocal claim: how roles switch depending on the reference point. De Beauvoir gives the example of a local who views others as foreigners until he himself sets out on a journey to find that now he is considered the foreigner. The book will help you step beyond the constraints of absolute meanings and bring out the relativity, reciprocity, and interdependency of the sexes as a condition for effective human interactions. This is, one of many, eye-opening insights for diversity management and negotiators of all sexes.

   Tip for negotiators: Do not accept to be the "second" sex when it comes to negotiations, no matter what your gender is.

2. **Mika Brzezinski,** *Know Your Value: Women, Money and Getting What You're Worth*

An inspiring and personal book with raw insights on navigating the business environment for professionals. The main benefit upon completion of the reading: an enhanced level of self-empowerment guaranteed to make you think twice before you ever again downplay your own value in any negotiation. The added benefit is that you will stop seeing yourself as your own worst enemy or your own toughest negotiation counterpart. Contains a noteworthy and timely warning for women who try to act like men at the negotiation table and vice versa.

Tip for negotiators: Know your value and claim it at the negotiation table (and in life).

3. **Barbara Annis, John Gray,** *Work with Me. How Gender Intelligence Can Help You Succeed at Work and in Life*

The assumptions of the bestselling book *Men are from Mars, Women are from Venus* adapted to the business world. This work discusses the notion of gender intelligence and shows how a synergy between the sexes can help achieve long-standing solutions both in business and beyond. It contains interesting insights into the blind spots of women and men and tips on how to bridge the different values. The work further examines how to build trust and establish credibility and exposes some of the communication pitfalls that often result in a battle of the sexes.

Tip for negotiators: Do not be the male or female negotiator. Be the smart negotiator.

CHAPTER 15

The Impact of Culture on Negotiation

CULTURE is the predominant system of values, beliefs, and patterns of behavior passed from one generation to the next, be it in families, countries, or companies. Negotiating in a multicultural environment requires understanding the key determinants of culture, such as language, history, social customs, traditions, and business practice. Many negotiators ask why they should make the effort to understand the cultural background of their counterpart. They wonder whether the other party should not bend to the rules of their culture instead. This approach places culture as one of the tokens in the power struggle—my culture is more important than yours, and we will follow its rules. This logic is faulty.

Intercultural sensitivity is an act of courtesy toward your negotiation partner and toward yourself. If you do not understand the intercultural differences and their impact on the negotiation process, you risk losing power, not gaining it. You might take things personally as an affront toward you as a person, whereas they might be culturally generic. This chapter will present the key factors that you need to take into account to boost your negotiation power in cross-cultural operations.

The first thing you will need to be aware of is that the definition of negotiation may differ depending on the culture. In some countries, negotiation is a fairly formalized process of information exchange between parties aimed at reaching mutually acceptable agreements. In others, negotiation is an attempt at gathering as much intelligence about the other party as possible, in order to advance the interests of your party. Negotiation can also be the last resort in conflict management when all other mechanisms have failed. When you set out to negotiate in a foreign country, it is recommended that you verify whether you and your partner are on the same thesaurus page, because the definition may shape the negotiation process.

Another factor that may seriously influence your bargaining power is understanding who is perceived as a legitimate negotiator. You will need to find out whether the choice is related to gender, seniority (age), or experience. Failure to do so might lead you to take things personally. For example, if you are a young female negotiator sent out on a business trip to a country where the negotiators are typically male, you might be overlooked at the negotiation table, which in turn will lead you to become defensive and assert your position more strongly, which can adversely affect both the task and the relationship. Sometimes, the best use of power is knowing when to step off the stage and manage the negotiation from behind the scenes.

Next on your cross-cultural negotiation checklist is understanding the nature of agreements. On the procedural level, this includes assessing the degree of formality: does the negotiation process follow a certain procedural framework, what is the protocol, are there any specific legal requirements that need to be fulfilled, how detailed should the terms of the agreement be, does it require a written form or is a gentleman's agreement valid, what is the time outlook of agreements: short versus long term. On the individual level, this step involves comprehending the attitudes toward risk of the parties (risk-avoidance level) and emotionalism—the extent to which the negotiators express emotions or display a poker face.

You will also need to equip yourself with knowledge of the business etiquette in the conduct of negotiations. It is helpful to know what are the practices that are related to the exchange of business cards, gift giving, accepting invitations to informal events, what is the dress code, food and drink preferences, and any other rituals that form part of the bonding process. If in doubt, follow the maxim, "When in Rome, do as the Romans." In high-stake intercultural negotiations, you might consider appointing the services of a cross-cultural translator who will help you navigate the overseas negotiation.

One of the other cultural differences that is worth mentioning is the approach to time, as this is also a commonly used negotiation tactic. We distinguish between polychronic and monochronic cultures.

Negotiators from polychronic cultures typically multitask and work on several projects simultaneously; consequently, their attention might be diluted. They manage interruptions and react well to change. Time runs freely for them, because their focus is on the task and not its timeframe. This may cause deadlines to shift and time schedules to be more flexible. Negotiators from monochronic cultures operate according to the opposite set of rules. They prefer to do one thing at a time, follow the agenda, and operate according to a linear timeframe.

You must, therefore, be able to differentiate whether you are dealing with a mono- or polychronic counterpart and adapt your approach accordingly. Secondly, you need to make sure whether the approach to time is culturally embedded or whether it is a tactic. For example, if you are a negotiator from a monochronic culture, you are most likely going to be agitated if your negotiation partner shows up late for your meeting, interrupts the negotiation to focus on different projects, and pushes deadlines. You might even consider the behavior as a sign of disrespect toward you. For example, one of my trainees from Germany was very offended when the meeting with the client during his business trip to Dubai, UAE, started late. He perceived this as a lack of respect for his time. When the reunion finally started, his performance was adversely affected because of this perceived affront. If you realize that it is a cultural characteristic, your reaction to it will be far less emotional than it would be if you were to consider it as a deliberate tactic to minimize your power at the negotiation table.

Let us now move on to the communication differences that may impact the negotiation process. Anthropologist E. T. Hall distinguished two types of cultures: low and high context. For the sake of simplicity, this chapter will only focus on the feature linked to communication: explicit or implicit information transfer. Negotiators from low-context cultures tend to explicitly transfer the message; there are no hidden meanings. Verbal communication is preferred, and there is limited recourse to non-verbal and para-verbal communication. Information exchange follows a logical and linear pattern. In high-context cultures, you will need to *read the air*, which means mastering the art of indirection and symbolism in the information-sharing process. Appointing a negotiator with a strictly one-sided low-context approach to communication to interact with a negotiator from a high-context culture is about as recommended as sending a bull to a china shop.

In many cross-cultural negotiations, you will notice an imbalance in the numbers of negotiators at either side of the table. Collectivist cultures emphasize the goals of the group over the interests of an individual. Consensus and group decision-making are common approaches. Multiparty gatherings are the social norm that is transplanted into business practice. The executives who are not aware of this cultural difference often ask whether strength is in the numbers: if they brought five people, should we bring ten? They perceive the collectivist dimension as a display of power. Provided it is not a tactic, the answer is that the smaller the negotiation team, the better. The more people you bring to the table, the more likelihood of divergences of opinion, conflict among the members, dilution of the negotiation objective, and disintegration of the negotiation strategy. Remember to strive for quality not quantity, and allow only the best negotiators to the table—those who are well trained tactically and have elevated standards of intercultural sensitivity.

Key takeaways:
1. Verify how you and your partner define negotiation.
2. Make sure you know who is perceived as a legitimate negotiator.
3. Understand the nature of agreements.
4. Equip yourself with knowledge on the negotiation etiquette.
5. Beware of the divergent approach to time.
6. Recognize the differences in communication (low- versus high-context culture).
7. Keep in mind that the number of negotiators might vary in collectivist and individualistic cultures.

Chapter 15: Further Reading

There are numerous studies and theories on the impact of culture on the negotiation process. Keep in mind that each theory should serve as a starting reference point. The analysis is not complete without individual profiling that takes into account the unique characteristics of your negotiation partner(s).

For a well-rounded preparation for intercultural negotiations, you can start with the following:

1. **Geert Hofstede,** *Cultures Consequences: Comparing Values, Behaviors, Institutions, and Organizations Across Nations*
   This is one of the classic studies on cultural differences developed in the 1970s. It will give you an understanding of the cultural values that affect business conduct across cultures: power distance, uncertainty avoidance, individualism and collectivism, masculinity and femininity, and long- versus short-term orientation.
   Note: the insights on the uncertainty avoidance (risk-taking patterns), power distance (acceptance of the fact that power is unequally distributed—hierarchy), and individualism (which translates, among others, to the frequent question of the number of participants at the negotiation table) are particularly interesting for a global negotiator.
   Tip for negotiators: Type in "Hofstede's cultural dimensions" in your browser. The search results will include a graphic representation of the dimensions and country comparison as an option. You can compare different countries when you prepare for a negotiation with representatives from several cultures.

2. **Erin Meyer,** *The Culture Map: Decoding How People Think, Lead, and Get Things Done Across Cultures*
   A comprehensive study of the communication patterns, value systems, and business customs from around the world enriched with insights on persuasion, decision-making power, and productive conflict management. The novel approach is the application of the concept of relativism of culture—when comparing cultures from the same cultural spectrum (such as China and Japan), that you might think are similar, you still need to identify those differences between them that will impact behavioral patterns.
   Tip for negotiators: Use the tool that Meyer proposes to plot your culture on the eight-scale framework. You will get a map that will allow you to compare your culture to the scales of your negotiation partner.

3. **Terri Morrison, Wayne A. Conaway, George A. Borden,** *Kiss, Bow or Shake Hands*

   A complete guide to doing business in 60 countries that includes cultural overviews, behavioral styles, negotiation techniques, business etiquette and practices, use of titles, gift-giving protocol, approach to time, dress codes, greetings, and gestures. Quick, easy, and digestible format.

   🤝 **Tip for negotiators:** Choose your country of interest and equip yourself with precious intercultural insights before your next negotiation.

4. **Edward Hall high- versus low-context cultures**

   For a speedy guide to the differences between how negotiators from different cultures behave: explicit versus implicit communication style, short- versus long-term focus, nature of relationships, and the existence of laws, you can do an Internet search by typing in "Hall high vs. low context cultures" in your browser.

   🤝 **Tip for negotiators:** The search results will provide you with another benchmark for your cross-cultural negotiations.

CHAPTER 16

Virtual Negotiation

CONDUCTING business remotely is the new reality. The COVID-19 crisis has caused a shift in the way business professionals communicate with each other. This chapter will focus on the three most frequent modes of e-negotiations: voice-based (telephone and videoconference) and text-based (instant messaging and e-mail). It is noteworthy that the technical part has not overgone a radical change. Negotiators still follow the traditional framework that encompasses agenda-setting, identification of the objective, preparation of the opening offer, consideration of options and alternatives, demand presentation and exchange, choice of approach, and execution of the negotiation strategy. What has changed is the relational part; consequently, it merits a more detailed analysis. The steps of preparing for a virtual negotiation are presented as follows.

1. Determine the negotiation objective
2. Profile your negotiation partner
3. Plan the approach, strategies and tactics
4. Design your virtual space
5. Prepare and empower yourself
6. Introduce rituals to strengthen the bond

Figure 16.12 Preparation grid for virtual negotiations

The main difference between a *normal* negotiation and a virtual one is the lack of face-to-face contact between the parties. This makes it more difficult to properly read your negotiation partner, a critical condition for building rapport. In order to better understand the person at the other end of the bandwidth, you will need to dedicate more effort to profiling described in Chapter 8. Some of the person-related barriers in virtual communication include accurate personality assessment and comprehending the mental map of the other person—the mosaic of cultural, environmental, experience-related, and individual elements that drive their behavior. A question often asked is whether we should use humor or emoticons to warm up the atmosphere in e-negotiations. The answer depends on how well you have done the profiling. Humor should be tailored to the human. There is nothing worse than a joke that is met with silence or an emoticon that is out of context or misinterpreted.

Another challenge you need to be aware of are perceptual errors, specifically perceptual selection and the synchrony bias. The former is related to the limitations of the attention span. The brain can only focus on selected pieces of information, so the question you need to ask yourself is how to channel the selective screening of your counterpart to what you want them to focus on. The synchrony bias relates to real-time information exchange (as in the case of phone or video-negotiations), as compared to the asynchrony of e-mail or text message exchange. Not getting a reply to a text message is an equivalent of the silence tactic used in face-to-face negotiations. Silence makes people uneasy and impatient. The main disadvantage of e-silence is that you cannot be sure whether your message was well received or if your counterpart is waiting you out. In order to avoid getting caught up in the vanishing virtual negotiator act, you should agree on a standard response period at the beginning of the negotiation before the tactics roll in.

The concept of synchrony leads to another vital aspect of virtual negotiations—time. In negotiations, timing and place are critical considerations. Have you ever made the right offer at the wrong time? If so, then you know how that ended. You need to use time to your advantage. In international negotiations, you will need to consider geographic time differences that affect business hours and weekend days. Furthermore, certain times of the day, such as before lunchtime, put you at risk of an encounter with a less receptive or distraught, or irritated partner. Furthermore, you will need to understand the individual time preferences of your counterpart—are they night owls or early birds (this will impact their attention spam at certain times of the day), do they have family obligations or individual routines that keep them occupied at certain moments of their day, and so on.

In terms of place, one must not neglect the importance of setting. Virtual negotiations may take place not only in business offices, but also from home offices. While the symbolic of the former is evident, the matter is more delicate when it comes to private settings. Conducting a videoconference from the comfort of your own home will affect your inner power status. Firstly, people tend to be more relaxed and *softer* in their private environments. This may make them more prone to making concessions. Secondly, what you display in the background is a substitute for the traditional power symbols that function externally.

Notice how experts in videoconferences like to record themselves with shelves filled with volumes of books behind them to imply the expertise power they have acquired. Companies that have their negotiators working from home during lockdowns will instruct them to use the company logo displays as the background. They know that the longer one looks at something, it becomes imprinted in the mind and gains legitimacy. A small investment for a strong persuasion tool. In terms of other tactics, some negotiators will deliberately sit with the light source behind them so that you cannot read their facial expressions clearly. Needless to say, attire and personal grooming also send a strong message about your role and position. Just like an actor in a theater does, design the virtual space to the effect you want to have on your negotiation partner.

Negotiating in virtual reality carries with it the danger of digital miscommunication. The majority of people do not have the ability to decipher the tone of an instant message or an e-mail correctly, although they assess their own skills as high. Some forget the permanent nature of virtual messages and the loss of control over who can read them.

In e-negotiations, alignment between the parties becomes more demanding. The exchanges tend to be more linear, less interactive, and less participative. On the relational level, you will need to create a bond by opening in a positive, action-oriented manner and building rapport before diving into the task. During voice-based negotiations, it is necessary that all parties have an equal opportunity to express themselves. Introduce a pattern of virtual respect and inclusion. When one side monopolizes the discussion, there may be personal resentment, which will increase the risk of precious information falling through the cracks.

Remember the 70:30 rule (listen: speak) and gather information on your negotiation partner. Say only what you want to uncover and not more. Never forget that anyone could be listening or registering you, so it is best to be risk-avoidant. In videoconferences, insist that the participants have their cameras on unless you want a more competitive dynamic. It is much easier to attack the little green light on your computer than a person, even if you see that person only on your screen.

Same as in the case of face-to-face negotiations, a virtual one does not end with an agreement being signed. A skilled negotiator needs to ensure the executability of the agreed-on terms. The major challenge is not the task itself, but the creation of the bond between the parties that will allow the task to be implemented. Naturally, rapport is more easily established when we see the person *live*: we observe the changes in their body language, as well as pick up on the subtle para-verbals. In business, many successfully concluded deals often begin and end with symbolic celebrations, such as a dinner or drinks (or a combination). You will need to adapt that business etiquette to your e-negotiations. Introduce and cultivate small rituals and make them an integral part of the negotiation process. This will differentiate you from all the other virtual personas.

Key takeaways:
1. Carefully check the accuracy of your profiling results, as you will be lacking face-to-face contact.
2. Tailor humor to the human.
3. Agree on a standard response time at the beginning of the negotiation to avoid virtual silence.
4. Pay attention to the right timing.
5. Craft your virtual background to your desired effect.
6. Beware that anything you do in virtual reality leaves a permanent record.

Chapter 16: Further Reading

Success in e-negotiations requires the grasping of the topic from three angles: the technical aspects related to virtual negotiating, the rules of global business conduct, and solid communication skills. Consequently, to equip yourself with a prep-kit for virtual negotiations, refer to the following:

1. **Nicholas Harkiolakis, Daphne Halkias, Sam Abadir,** *e-Negotiations. Networking and Cross-Cultural Business Transactions*
A useful toolkit for remote negotiations with an introduction to technology, online intelligence, and tips for remote dealmaking. I specifically recommend Chapter 6, which deals with communication modes, the advantages and disadvantages of synchronous and asynchronous technologies, as well as main communication mediums for e-negotiations.

   Tip for negotiators: Get up to speed on the latest technological advances. Use the tools of modern technology to your advantage in order to succeed in your e-negotiations.

2. **Jeanne M. Brett,** *Negotiating Globally. How to Negotiate Deals, Resolve Disputes, and Make Decisions Across Cultural Boundaries*
A technical framework that will help you and your team better prepare for global negotiations. This book will allow you to understand the intercultural differences and procedural norms that impact negotiations. It presents three strategic models for negotiating in cross-cultural teams.

   Tip for negotiators: Remember that the smaller the negotiation team, the more control you have over it. Have proper decision-making procedures in place, clearly designate responsibility lines, and introduce conflict resolution mechanisms to avoid *the wisdom of the herd* and intercultural pitfalls.

3. **Alan Barker,** *Improve Your Communication Skills*
A practical guide to enhancing the effectiveness of your virtual business communication skills. It provides tips on how to properly structure e-mails, how to craft presentations by following Monroe's Motivation Sequence (Page 111), and on how to deliver persuasive messages by appealing to the three elements of character: reason (ethos), logic (logos), and passion (pathos).

   Tip for negotiators: Apply the tool of influence RASCAL (reciprocity, authority, scarcity, consistency, alignment, and liking) to enhance your virtual negotiation prowess.

CHAPTER 17

Negotiation is a Mirror

THE mirror reflects perceived reality; it is a powerful tool that can be used either for deception or mental seduction. What you display in terms of self-assurance, inner status, and authority reflects in the actions of your counterpart and ultimately affects their willingness to cooperate with you.

The traditional approach to negotiation revolves around the use of tactics and power plays against the other party. However, it neglects the importance of self-management with the aim of creating attachment and bonding, the critical elements on the path to reaching real and long-lasting agreements. You need to abandon the short-sighted focus on technical execution alone, and instead focus on the interplay between the three constituents presented in Figure 17.13.

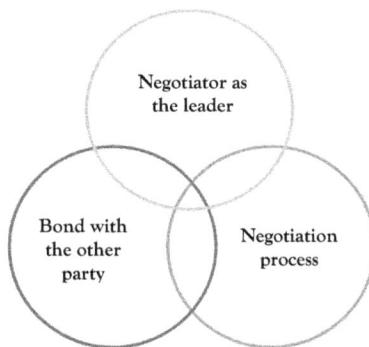

Figure 17.13 The mirror negotiation cycle

The negotiation process does not commence when two parties meet at the negotiation table. It starts with you and your power of focus. You are the leader and the one who will lay down the fundaments for the negotiation and for how the process will unfold. Your external preparation will involve the tactical and strategic steps described in the previous chapters. Simultaneously, you will be preparing yourself internally: strengthening your inner bargaining power, channeling your emotional energy toward the desired outcome, and managing your ego. You will be the one leading the negotiation, but in order for your counterpart to follow, you will need to understand their objectives and system of pertinence (which you will have achieved by profiling). A true leader empowers their followers. You will do this by including the other party in the process and guiding them elegantly by framing their options. You will sketch the roadmap leading the negotiation toward a common goal. Remember that, by nature, people will follow, provided that they believe that they have a choice and are following out of their own will.

In order to secure commitment to the task, you will need to build attachment and create a bond between you and your negotiation partner. According to the feedback I collected while working with executives, students, and the United Nations (UN) officials, trust is the fundament of any relationship, business, or personal. A synergy between driving the process and managing the emotional factor allows to create high energy. Trust is built by working together and overcoming certain challenges jointly. Its main tool is open and inclusive communication between the parties.

Words are like weapons; sometimes, they can cut through the relationship. If used wisely, they can mentally seduce your partner to an agreement. It is, therefore, worth mentioning some of the most common verbal mistakes that happen in negotiations. The first one is the famous "yes, but (…)" phrase. As soon as we hear the word *but*, we know that the *yes* has no value. Why use it then?

The next example is very toxic and involves references to honesty and trust. Let it be known that a person who has sincere intentions does not need to pull out the honesty card. Imagine a situation in which you set a meeting to negotiate a salary increase with your boss. You enter the room and as soon as you sit down, you are confronted with the following question: "You trust me, right?" What should you reply? Instinctively, you know that this is a tricky question. If you say yes, then you pass over the cards to them; the task part is compromised. If you negate, then you risk ruining the relationship. The best solution in such cases is to direct the discussion back to the agenda or the objective of the meeting. You can respectfully reply that you value their time and the topic of the meeting is your raise and not trust. This is the recommended advice in many situations when the other party tries to attack or manipulate you.

The next category of trust-killers is the subjective stance. Phrases such as: "You must understand that (…)," "We are making you a generous offer," or "Let me tell you how it's going to be" indicate a one-sided focus. Hardly the ideal conditions for establishing trust. Telling your counterpart that they must do something is guaranteed to have them do…the exact opposite. Qualifying your proposal or offer with adjectives shows you are trying to convince yourself. What you perceive as generous, fair, great, and so on is not necessarily understood as such by your counterpart. Speaking of fairness, refrain from using the "It's not fair!" argument, unless you are in your teenager rebellious phase. The "let me tell you how it's going to be" is a great phrase if you want to get into a deadlock at the outset during which both parties, or rather their egos, will get into a contest on who will show whom how it will be.

Building a bond with your negotiation partner requires you to be able to see things from their perspective. This does not mean that you agree, but you should show empathy. Avoid passing on judgments and assessing the situation from your viewpoints and according to your system of values. Everyone is unique and desperately wants to be treated as such. Avoid generalizations, such as "Salespeople, women, men (…) are always pushy, emotional, ego driven (…)."

Lastly, managing emotions requires more than just telling someone to *calm down*. In fact, this phrase will certainly draw their attention to the fact that they are destabilized and will give the negative feeling legitimacy; it will also cause a defensive reaction to counter having been told what to do.

Do not limit your own bargaining power by asking if you may add something to the discussion, apologizing for contributing or disturbing, or using the minimizing words *just* or *only*: "I only wanted to say (…)," "just a small note (…)." Believe that you are a valid voice at the negotiation table, and others will see and treat you as such.

The power of dialogue should be channeled toward building bridges through common understanding. Detoxification and reframing will be helpful tools in the exchanges with your negotiation partner.

Remember that the same thing can be expressed in at least two different ways depending on the effect you want to have.

Craft the image that you want your negotiation partner to reflect by addressing the three elements: self-management (you), the negotiation process (the task), bond with the other party (the relationship). The mirror effect will enable you to achieve longevity in your negotiations.

Key takeaways:
1. Do not focus only on technical execution.
2. Establish yourself as the leader—lay down the fundaments for the negotiation process.
3. Empower yourself internally.
4. Involve the other party in the process by giving them a choice.
5. Build attachment and create a bond between you and your negotiation partner.
6. Avoid toxic words and phrases.
7. Address the three elements: self-management (you), the negotiation process (the task), bond with the other party (the relationship).

Chapter 17: Further Reading

Value in negotiations is about more than just the attribution of a monetary amount. While the achievement of the task is an indisputable goal, it is only an extrinsic factor—it brings value but does not *add* value. External rewards flow from the outside, as opposed to intrinsic factors, which originate inside of the negotiator. The latter have a stronger motivational impact, which is reflected in the behavior of the other party. Here is a guide to value-adding negotiations:

1. **Frans De Waal, *The Age of Empathy***
   Human brains are hardwired to form a neural interconnected network. We unconsciously mimic other people's behavior, our *feeling* brain can identify with the emotions felt by the other person, we even have the ability to send telepathic vibes. This book sheds new insights on the popular and widely used phrase "someone else's shoes." Discover what this really means and how you can fill those shoes and walk toward successful negotiations.

🤝 **Tip for negotiators:** Radiate empathy and watch how it reflects back to you. Create value for yourself and your negotiation partner, it will pay off with a premium.

2. **Ndaba Mandela, *11 Life Lessons from Nelson Mandela***

"We all have the power to change our story." Amending yours will inevitably alter the dynamic between you and the people you interact with. This book is a collection of personal memories of Nelson Mandela. Each lesson unfolds precious truths that will leave a lasting imprint of self-empowerment in the mind of the reader.

🤝 **Tip for negotiators:** Powerlessness is a barrier in your own mind. You alone have the power to change how you perceive the negotiation. Use that power to make up an image you will be proud to look at in the mirror of negotiation.

3. **Robert H. Mnookin, Scott R. Peppet, Andrew S. Tulumello, *Beyond Winning. Negotiating to Create Value in Deals and Disputes***

Contrary to what many negotiators set out for in their interactions, negotiation is about more than just winning. What does *beyond* winning mean? The authors of this book uncover the challenges of dealmaking and the tensions related to creating and distributing value. They present a problem-solving approach in view of resolving disputes and ethical dilemmas that may occur between the parties.

🤝 **Tip for negotiators:** The secret recipe for a truly successful negotiation is the combination of empathy and assertiveness.

CHAPTER 18

Negotiation Booster

To succeed in a negotiation, you need to leverage the task-related aspects with the underlying emotional factors. The task part consists of what is often globally referred to as the negotiation toolkit: the strategy, approach, and tactics. You need to master these technical aspects to a level that becomes second nature. The more adept you are with the tools, the less stressed and emotional you will get when you need to apply them. This will allow you to channel your energy. However, even the best craftsperson will not excel if they fail to manage their emotions, ego, and stress in a negotiation. Self-empowerment, perception management, and the use of impression management techniques are what give the toolkit momentum and allows you to thrive in your negotiations. To help boost your inner bargaining power, the *Negotiation Booster* approach breaks down the negotiation process into four phases: Primer, Shadowing, Sealer, Implementor.

In the Primer phase, you will focus on how you can achieve your most desired negotiation outcome by priming your mind for success before your next important negotiation. Tell yourself that failure is not an option, although you have alternatives. This will include strategic preparation, channeling your emotions into achieving your desired goal, and boosting your inner bargaining power. Two helpful tools are visualization and the retro-flash technique. The former relates to imagining the outcome and the resulting anticipatory emotions, a potent motivational instrument. The retro-flash is when you recall an event from your past that you consider your moment of glory. It can be anything: the day you met the love of your life, landing your dream job, making it in a new city, or any other super-empowering experience. Remember how you felt then, how the limits to what you thought you could achieve ceased to exist. Now let your remembering-self guide you toward your future desired outcome, project the past bliss to the next event to duplicate its success.

The Shadowing phase is designed to help you avoid tunnel vision when the negotiation starts. You can approach this phase in two ways. You can either have an external objective party by your side (an appointed negotiation expert, a trusted adviser, a mentor, a negotiation trainer, or an impartial colleague) or you can act as your own shadow, provided you are skilled enough to go to the emotional balcony. While you negotiate, your shadow should make sure that you stay focused on the execution of the negotiation strategy established in the Primer phase, regardless of the tactics that may be used against you. Regardless of whether you benefit from external support or rely on yourself, the trick is the ability to distance yourself from the action in order to see the big picture and react in a rational manner.

While the Primer is future-oriented, the Sealer has a more retrospective outlook. In this phase, you identify how to avoid costly mistakes and how to never make the same one (nor a variation of it) twice. Based on your real-life experiences, you assess your past negotiation outcomes, review the types of challenges you faced (both tactical and emotional), and identify areas for future improvement. In order to do this, I recommend that you make a short self-debrief after each negotiation by asking yourself one simple question: if I could do it again, what would I do differently? You will see a pattern of behavior emerge that will give you an idea of the problematic area. Based on your findings, you can set up a tailor-made strategy for your future negotiations.

A negotiation does not end with a deal being signed. This is what differentiates a dealmaker from a real-maker negotiator. The former has a high volume of signed paperwork, which does not necessarily translate into long-lasting and executable agreements. The Implementor is the last step in your self-empowerment journey. The key focus here is the assessment of the implementation of the agenda, strategy, and the objectives you set out to achieve. This is where you execute the task. On the emotional level, you should celebrate your achievements. Do not just mentally move on to the next task; take a moment to recognize your successes. Let them be your source of strength for your future negotiations, as they become the basis for your next retro-flash moment.

Provided you take time to go through the four stages, you will develop a perceptual set (a pattern of future behavior based on past experiences) characterized by an elevated level of self-control, confidence, and bargaining power that will radiate from within you. A successful mind-set attracts success in the business arena and beyond. Your negotiator partner will sense the magical aura surrounding you and will react accordingly to it.

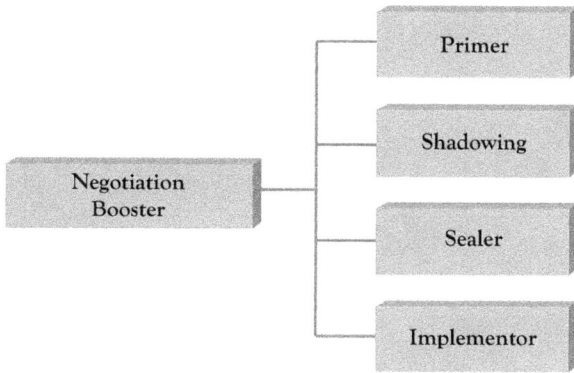

Figure 18.14 The four phases of the Negotiation Booster approach

Key takeaways:
1. Leverage the task-related aspects with the underlying emotional factors.
2. Manage your emotions, ego, and stress.
3. Tell yourself that failure is not an option.
4. Use visualization and the retro-flash technique.
5. Distance yourself from the action.
6. Perform a self-debrief after each negotiation.
7. Execute the task and celebrate your achievements.
8. Adopt all the phases: Primer, Shadowing, Sealer, Implementor in your negotiation approach.

PART II

Negotiation Booster Sealer

Now that you primed yourself for achieving success in your negotiations, we can move on to some practical examples from international business practice. This part is a recollection of the experiences I compiled while interacting with other business professionals during negotiation meetings at the United Nations and while conducting negotiation trainings at some of the biggest companies from Europe, Asia, the Middle East, and the United States.

While writing this part, I searched in my memory (and notes) for the most common mistakes that negotiators tend to make. Although parents would like it to be otherwise, one cannot completely avoid the mistakes of others. However, what we can do is heighten our awareness of certain dynamics that may tip the scales of the negotiation in our favor. The added value of reading about the adventures of others is that you feel more secure in not being the only one who sometimes stumbles. Following what one of the executives in a training once told me: you can relate better to the mistakes of others.

One of the negotiation maxims is the concept of going to the emotional balcony, the safe place in your mind that allows you to take mental distance from the action. Consider this part as your intellectual balcony. The eight short cases that follow will equip you with insightful tips on how to navigate around real-life challenges and boost your negotiation power. They are designed to seal the theoretical aspects and bridge them with practical application.

CASE 1

The Redline Documents
Power Struggle

DURING one particularly long and complex negotiation of a future joint venture between a company based in Dubai and a firm in Paris, I found my creativity as a negotiation facilitator taken to the test. The cultural differences evident in the divergent approach to time and the negotiation process itself, as well as the exhaustion from the back and forth communication (characterized by completely different styles of the high- and low-context cultures) were clouding the chances of closure in the foreseeable future. After lengthy discussions and many exchanges of redline documents, the representatives of the two companies came to a standstill. We ran the risk of the deal falling through. Eager to overcome the blockage, I went over the details of what was discussed up to that point. I could not find any serious barriers to agreement, such as legal, administrative, or financial obstacles. In short, the analyses and due diligence clearly showed that both parties objectively shared a common goal: the setting up of the joint venture in view of internationalization of their activities. I came to the conclusion that what was missing in order to conclude the agreement was the full understanding and engagement of both parties in the process.

I, therefore, decided to schedule a meeting with the representatives of both parties on neutral territory, in a meeting room at Frankfurt airport where both could fly in and out after the reunion. My role was to act as an intermediary between the two parties. I came well prepared and with a concrete goal to move things forward. The aim of the meeting was to present the soft copy of the documents with the changes proposed by the Paris team to the partner from Dubai, which would then hopefully push the discussions forward. When we all arrived, the parties chose where they would sit. Not surprisingly under the circumstances of blockage, the two partners chose seats opposite each other. This was not a good start for overcoming a deadlock and steering toward a more cooperative dynamic.

I decided to try out a little experiment on them. I set up my workspace and started looking for the latest version of the agreement that only I had. After a moment, I looked up and said: "It seems our secretary forgot to pack enough copies for us all. I only have one copy here with me. Would you mind sharing it?" To my surprise, the partners agreed to this without hesitation. Immediately they sat side by side to facilitate the work with one document between them. After all, neither wanted to be at a disadvantage by having to read the document upside down. Shoulder to shoulder with two pens in different colors and one contract version, the parties engaged in the process of discussing the terms and proposing modifications that could be acceptable for both companies. The atmosphere quickly changed from confrontational to cooperative, both in the room setting and in spirit.

We managed to overcome the impasse in the course of just one workday. What was the secret behind this sudden change in dynamics? It was the engagement of the parties, in the sense that both proposed changes and discussed them instead of sending *my version* and *your version* back and forth. More importantly, in this interaction, nothing was imposed, but rather it was a process of two-sided ownership in a quest for the best possible solution that would push the deal forward.

This situation taught me a few valuable lessons that day that I pass on to the executives whom I train. Finding a common objective can be challenging, especially if both counterparts only see their side of the transaction. A negotiation is a relation of interdependency between two people: I need you, and you need me to close the deal. A critical condition for engagement is for the counterpart to firstly feel understood and respected. Many executives erroneously think that granting the courtesy of understanding and respect is a sign of weakness. On the contrary, the party who can manage their emotions, keep an open mind, set the tone as well as the expectations is the one who drives the process. Furthermore, understanding is the key to gathering information and, on that basis, identifying what the objectives of your counterpart are. This then allows choosing the right strategy and tactics for the execution of the negotiation. It is vital to avoid imposing solutions; rather the other party should feel that they have been involved, under your carefully thought-through guidance, in the process. Involvement in the decision-making process reduces the risk of the terms of the agreement being broken.

The preceding example uncovers one other interesting fact. The moment executives exchange redline versions, they develop the endowment effect. Even if the goal is to reach an agreement, they become opponents: my version against your version of the document. Neither wants to let their version go. This often leads to a deadlock. Should this be the case, it is recommended to apply creative solutions for engaging both parties. Such solutions should fall outside of the standard set of negotiation tactics or, worse yet, manipulation that the other party can see through and naturally be discouraged by. The best ones seem to be those that rely on natural, instinctive reactions, such as sitting side by side over one set of documents. Certainly, one can think of other such ideas for remote interactions.

CASE 2

What Lies Beneath the Iceberg Tip

THE urban negotiation myth is the story of two sisters who are arguing over the distribution of one orange. Both want the fruit. They spend a lot of time and energy on exchanging arguments who should get it. In the end, they fail to find the most efficient resolution of their problem. They end up cutting the orange in half. As it later turns out, one sister wanted to make orange juice, and the other needed the peel of the orange to add flavor to a cake she was baking. Under these circumstances, satisfying the needs of one sister did not exclude or even limit the satisfaction of the needs of the other. What was the problem then? They both stayed locked in their positions and all their energy was directed at defending them. Eventually, this led to a phenomenon that is referred to as *tunnel vision*. Just like the light in the tunnel narrows, so does the ability of the parties to see beyond their rigid demands. Once this happens, creating options other than one-sided becomes difficult.

It is fairly easy to find out what the position of the other party is. The *what do you want* (at least in monetary terms) often surfaces when the first offer is made. This opening proposal, if carefully crafted, then serves as an anchor to the subsequent negotiation. When preparing the opening offer, it is, therefore, vital to take the time to gather useful information in order to choose an anchoring closest to the other party's barely acceptable terms and to be able to justify it with objective criteria. Excessive anchoring, understood as the risk of asking more than our partner finds reasonable, may lead to either the chilling (loss of interest in the negotiation) or the boomerang (an equally excessive counteroffer) effect and ruin the negotiation at the outset. The mitigation of this risk alone does not guarantee a successful negotiation. All it ensures is that the process kicks off.

The opening offer can thus be considered as the *what* part of the equation. However, in order to maximize the limited resource and lead to an agreement that has the potential for durability, the parties have to explore both the *what* and the *why* questions. Instead of focusing on their positions—the "What do you want?"—the orange sisters could have investigated the motives driving these positions and asked one simple question: "Why do you want it?" Interests and positions can best be mentally illustrated by the example of an iceberg. Positions are above the waterline, while interests are below. Interests are driven by, among others, individual needs and preferences. At any point in time, human behavior is driven by a continuum of needs, according to Maslow's theory. It is the role of a skilled negotiator to dive in and grasp the understanding of the whole picture.

Many executives seek advice on how to proceed with exploring the interests behind the positions expressed by their counterparts. A negotiation is not a confession, and asking the *why* question point blank will seldom be awarded with the true reasons. Books on communication repeatedly suggest asking open questions. This is a half-solution. It is a good strategy, in the sense that it will unveil information about the other person. People reveal themselves in talking. Their choice of words and what they express is an indication of many factors: their personality, attitude, emotional state, intellectual standing, intercultural sensitivity, moral and ethical standards, education level, social class, international exposure, and many other aspects. By intentional listening, it is possible to understand the mental map of the other party—their inner Global Positioning System (GPS) that directs the behavior. The more one uncovers, the easier it becomes to understand what drives the behavior of our counterpart and what motivates them. It is, thus, important to ask open questions that are directed toward achieving a specific goal, not just shooting open questions. One needs to be careful in order not to design and pose questions that serve the confirmation bias. The point of the exercise is to uncover new information, not to confirm what one thinks they already know. The best way is to keep an open ear(s) and assume we never know enough.

Intentional listening with the aim of understanding the interests behind the verbalized position means hearing not only the words, but also the contextualization of behavior. It calls for a paradigm shift on the part of the *interest investigator*—the ability to see the different angles of a given subject. Power and status symbols, the choice of profession, and type of lifestyle are all helpful indicators in profiling our counterpart and grasping the meaning of why they are making a specific demand.

CASE 3

Labels are a Self-Fulfilling Prophecy

TYPICALLY, we tend to equate the difficulties we face with the person we are dealing with. If we cannot get what we want, we often tend to attribute the fault to the personality traits of the other person (she is stubborn, he always needs to have things done his way, she cannot control her emotions, he is too competitive, and so on). Hence, so many books have been written on managing *difficult people* and conducting difficult conversations. Pointing a finger at the other person is certainly easier than admitting that the process is negatively impacted by our own shortcomings, perception errors, or flawed logic. The core of the issue is the inability to separate the people, including ourselves, from the problem.

The trend to turn the tables, or rather the mirror, around is budding in the literature on negotiation. It is being recognized that long-term negotiations require achieving a triple win: the classic win–win between the two parties supported by an individual (internal) win. In my seminars, I teach the participants that the first step to negotiation is not preparation, as many other negotiation books suggest, but rather self-preparation. Any negotiation should start with self-management: taking control of one's emotions, automatic impulses, unconscious reactions, ego, and embedded patterns of learned behavior. If one cannot manage their own self and apply rational thinking free of judgment, prejudices, bias, and stereotypes, then the chances of balancing the task and relationship part of the negotiation process are highly unlikely.

Why is drawing a line between people and oneself and the problem so important? Firstly, it frees up the mental energy that should be directed at finding a joint solution to the distribution arrangement that both parties are sharing. Secondly, doing so does not detriment the relationship between the parties, a crucial yet very elusive element of sustainable agreements. Thirdly, it does not cloud the logic like excessive reliance solely on emotions might.

Separating the people from the problem can be achieved by managing emotions. Emotions are like our internal Global Positioning System (GPS); they cannot and should not be switched off. Nonetheless, they need to be kept under guard. The human brain is built in such a way that when the external trigger enters, we first feel, then we think. It is, therefore, physically not possible to be emotional and rational at the same time.

Based on the stories shared by the executives I trained, here are some tips on how to deal with people who are trying to intimidate or threaten us by making personal attacks rather than concentrating on the dilemma. The most important is to break the cycle between success and intimidation and instead to consciously steer the discussion toward the negotiation goal. This can be achieved by not reacting to behavior we find unacceptable or simply by asking for a break to calm down. Many executives question whether asking for a break when things get heated will not be seen as a weakness on their part. Quite the contrary, it is wiser to take a moment off than make a decision that will be regretted later. This approach is not to be mistaken with avoidance, which is simply doing nothing. The time-out technique is referred to as "going on the emotional balcony." The balcony designates a place, away from the main stage of the negotiation events, where we can cool off and look at the situation from a fresh perspective. My training experience shows that distancing oneself constitutes one of the main difficulties for many people. As one of the participants recently said during one of our sessions when we were talking about the emotional balcony: "I don't think I've ever been there before." Have you?

Once back from the balcony, we can express our feelings without sending the other side on a guilt or anger trip. Instead of criticizing, becoming defensive, or making personal attacks, it is recommended to describe how we feel. Each person has the right to express how something feels. A nice formula that can be recommended is as follows: "I feel (express emotion) when you do (define act/behavior) because (reason)." Focusing on the problem and not on the person can best be done by making the other party understand that they will obtain what they want only by negotiating on the merits of the case. It is often helpful to steer the discussion back to the common objective of the negotiation.

Finally, a good technique may also be posing an open question in a deliberate effort to involve the other party in the process: "How can we achieve our common goal?" This empowers the other party and allows them to take ownership of the process, under our reigns.

A common mistake that executives make is labeling: this is a difficult client, tricky account, tough negotiation, and so on. The moment you internally or externally label the negotiation as challenging, it has just become twice as difficult. This is the effect of subjective priming. The emotions will be activated for expected difficulties, and the level of stress hormones will rise. Rational reactions are at risk of being limited or overlooked. This is not to say that preparation should not include the anticipation of obstacles that will inevitably cause certain difficulties to surface. This is part of the negotiation game, or any human interaction for that matter. The trick is to take it for what it is and not add to the distress by attributing negative labels.

CASE 4

Do Not Split the Cake, Bake a Larger One

THIS example is best illustrated by reference to one of the classics of negotiation simulation cases established and taught at the Program on Negotiation (PON) at Harvard Law School. The case involves the sale of a vintage automobile.[8] The car is a unique one; it is in top shape, has recently undergone a refurbishment, and has only been used for short country escapades by its rich owner who prides himself on his collection of luxury vehicles. The potential buyer is a wealthy widow who recently experienced the death of her husband, a very controlling man who liked to take all the decisions on their behalf. She sees the car during her vacation and immediately falls in love with it. She sends her representative to negotiate the terms of the transaction with the secretary of the owner. The widow has a budget of 55,000 to 65,000 U.S. dollars. The seller's desired price for this unique car is 60,000 to 70,000 U.S. dollars. In financial terms, there exists a zone of possible agreement (ZOPA)—the overlap between the most the buyer is willing to pay and the least the seller is willing to accept.

This imaginary negotiation is a reflection of a real-life one; it includes both subjective and objective factors. One of the subjective elements is the principal–agent relationship. Both the widow and the car owner have representatives acting on their behalf. These individuals have their own stakes in the negotiation: they are responsible for the outcome of the negotiation (its success or failure, the negotiated price and any additional extras, and so on), they wish to please their agents and prove their self-worth in the process. The seller and buyer are also driven by subjective forces. The widow has a desire to finally make her own decisions and not

---

[8] https://www.pon.harvard.edu/shop/bentley-convertible/

be taken for a fool while at it. The car owner wants the car to go to good hands. Naturally, both want the best price too.

As discussed earlier, one of the conditions of a sustainable agreement is the exploration of the interests behind the positions. However, unlike in the anecdote about the orange sisters, this negotiation involves more than just distributing (or ideally maximizing) the limited resource. What differentiates it is the fact that a monetary value has to be assigned and accepted in order to even consider maximizing the benefits for both parties. Ironically, if the agents get caught up solely in the subjective elements, specifically their own motivations and those of their principles, they run the risk of going into positional bargaining, rather than applying the principled approach. Positional bargaining would mean setting a price based purely on the subjective value of the transaction to each party. Naturally, we tend to overestimate the real value of things that are special for us; this is the aforementioned endowment effect in action. One of the ways to avoid foggy judgment is by referring to objective criteria: the market value of similar vehicles, the type of refurbishment work performed, the number of labor hours spent, the cost of replacement parts, and so on in order to establish a fair price for the automobile. Failure to refer to objective criteria will lead to a time- and energy-consuming battle of subjective arguments. This is hardly a constructive dynamic.

The second step on the road to reaching an agreement would be the creation of options that maximize the ZOPA. Here, a savvy negotiator makes room for the subjective elements that are important from the point of view of both parties. This is where the demands are introduced. A negotiation is an exercise in trade, the counterparts exchange something of less value for something of more value. By making space for the subjective elements in the transaction, the agents secure both the task and the relationship, which allows them not only to close the transaction, but possibly also open the gates to future cooperation. In the fictional negotiation example, the creative options could involve among others inviting the widow and her friends (other potential buyers) to a special show of other vintage cars on the part of the seller or a commitment to bring her friends to see the showcased vehicles on the part of the buyer. The sky is the limit when it comes to crafting creative options.

The challenges that executives encounter regarding the opportunities of expanding the resource relate to the limited demands that they bring to the table. Before each negotiation, it is recommended to prepare a list of demands and rank them according to the level of their importance. This helps to systemize the chips for trade and earmark those that can be used for making concessions (not to be confused with compromise). From my experience, business professionals prepare too few demands. They limit their own options before the negotiation even starts. Even worse, they take away their own bargaining power, because the party that brings demands to the table is ultimately the one that drives the negotiation. In other words, failure to place demands and think of creative options for their acceptance is a serious barrier to achievement of the negotiation objective. One might wonder why this mistake occurs. Creativity takes time, energy, and mental effort. One of my training participants asked me once: "Can we afford to spend time on preparing demands and then creating options for expanding the pie?" My answer was: can you afford not to?

I also observed that even if the executives prepare a set of demands, they lack conviction when they present them to the counterpart. The standard behaviors include expressing them with hesitation, doubt, an apologetic tone, as a shy request, as a question, or with a shower of justifications that directly follows. The moment you justify is the moment that you send the other party a signal that you do not believe that you deserve something. Predators strike at the sign of weakness. If you do not believe it yourself, why would the other party grant you that courtesy? Consequently, a lot of time is spent in trainings on making the participants feel that they have a legitimate right to make demands. Surprisingly, this is the part that makes people the most uncomfortable. This feeling of discomfort triggered by making a demand will naturally reduce the creative capabilities. Excessive stress reduces the ability to think *outside of the box*.

There is Always an Alternative

OPTIONS are created *inside* the negotiation with the other party either jointly in the form of a brainstorming session or via an individual exploration of potential solution(s). The beauty of creative options is that both parties can receive some benefits from incorporating them into the negotiation process. This fits well with the spirit of the mutual gains approach. Nonetheless, real-life negotiation is seldom an exercise in philanthropy. Although the ideal negotiation outcome is characterized by an optimized and applicable agreement, a better relationship between the parties, no resentment or bitterness, a feeling of shared satisfaction, and a desire to do business again, it should also be better than the alternatives or the cost of nonagreement. This Plan B is referred to as the best alternative to a negotiated agreement (BATNA). BATNA should not be mistaken with creative options. The latter are used to bridge the gap in case of lack of a zone of possible agreement (ZOPA) when both parties nonetheless want to conclude an agreement, for example, in cases when the relationship is more important than the financial merits. The best alternative is created *outside* the negotiation—it is the fallback position in case the negotiation fails; as such, it can be implemented unilaterally.

One of the things that I learned while watching my lawyer mom prepare her clients for court proceedings was the importance of mental empowerment. She meticulously went over the details of each case, but a great part of her efforts went into crafting and strengthening the clients' alternatives, in case things would not go the way they planned in court. The result: her clients walked into the courtroom with an aura of confidence and inner strength resulting from the fact that they had (or believed to have) an ace up their sleeve. She was rewarded with a very high success rate of the cases she won.

In the course of my negotiation practice, I have observed that the worst thing to do is to enter the negotiation with an "I have a knife on my throat" attitude, depicting that it is either this or nothing for me in this negotiation. Following my mom's example, the first thing I, therefore, do when I prepare my clients for important negotiations is to boost their inner bargaining power by helping them realize that there are always alternatives. They either already exist or need to be crafted. In this case, it is recommended to "bite more than you can chew." The more the alternatives, the greater the confidence.

Executives often have difficulties with believing in their alternatives. The result: they enter the negotiation with a palpable aura of self-doubt, which is immediately visible to their counterpart. Here are a few practical tips on how to design a back-up plan that have been successfully field-tested by the executives I trained. Firstly, identify all the plausible things you might do without the other party, in case you are unable to reach an agreement. Once this is done, calculate the value associated with each alternative. Select which of these alternatives is best...this is your BATNA.[9] Remember to always try to anticipate and analyze the other parties' BATNAs with equal care and objectivity. Strongly believe that your alternatives are valid. Make it known to the other party that you have external options but never reveal your real BATNA. Finally, believe that you are still the best alternative for your negotiation partner. If this were not the case, they would not be at the negotiation table!

---

[9] Thompson, L. 2008. The Truth About Negotiations. Dorchester: Pearson Education Limited.

CASE 6

Communicate to Win

PERFORMANCE review ratings consistently indicate ineffective communication as the main reason for managerial failure. A negotiation is nothing else than the attempt to introduce a new project—a proposal to maximize the limited resource by distributing it in such a way as to harness one's own interests and those of the other party. Communication is the only means of conveying that offer. Effective communication should work on three levels: verbal (words, content), nonverbal (appearance, gestures, body language, physical distance, bodily reactions), and para-verbal (flow, tone, intonation, pitch of voice, accents, latency period between words, silence). For it to be perceived as authentic, there has to be a balance between all three levels.[10] This means that the recipient will only perceive the message as real if there is no dissonance—the spoken message reflects the non- and para-verbal behavior of the speaker. In that sense, effective communication is an art of perception management. As stated by Jung, perception is the only reality. People react based on their perceptions of reality, not reality itself.

Perception should, therefore, be crafted on two levels: internally and externally. We can stage the impact we want to have on the other person by careful choice of words, the way in which we convey our demands, and by paying attention to body language. Internally, the challenge is linked to managing the negative emotions related to the anticipation of rejection, which is at the source of rejection's destructive power. The paralyzing fear of rejection far too often governs how (or whether at all) we verbalize our proposals and how the other person perceives them.

The importance and breadth of communication merits a separate study. For the purposes of this chapter, I will only concentrate on the

[10] Morgan, N., 2013. *How to Become an Authentic Speaker.* HBR's 10 Must Reads on Communication, Harvard Business Review Press, Boston, Massachusetts.

aspects that pertain to the skills effective negotiators should consider, including in their bargaining repertoire, in order to avoid the risk of failure of their negotiating efforts.

The saying "He who complies against his will is of his opinion still" shows that people do not react well to imposed solutions, states, or world-views of others. Consequently, telling your counterpart that they must understand something sends a dual message: of enforcing combined with underestimating their mental capability. This is a recipe for an immediate defensive attitude, which will make navigating toward a more cooperative path more challenging.

Another common mistake that executives make is presenting and evaluating an offer from their own perspective or offering subjective solutions too quickly without having heard out and understood the other party. It is not possible to modify an attitude by telling someone to change or do something. In order to impact the behavior, one needs to first address the affective, and then the cognitive elements in the system that makes up an attitude. When an external trigger enters the brain, people first feel (the amygdala reacts), then they think and rationalize, and finally act. Therefore, our judgments and choices are nothing else than a reflection of endorsed and rationalized feelings. A skilled negotiator understands that the aim of communication—to influence people's behavior—can only be obtained by respecting the feel–think–act sequence.

Many negotiators struggle to find the best arguments to support their offer and the demands they are making. They waste a lot of time and energy on producing reasons to support their positions. In doing so, they are only really convincing themselves and their egos. The other party will inevitably reciprocate by pulling out their artillery of arguments. The result is a never-ending debate that ultimately causes both parties to lose sight of the objective of the negotiation. In some cases, this may lead to an emotional spiral of attack and defense or criticism and justification. With reference to the attitudinal aspects resulting from the brain struc-ture, it is not possible to be emotional and rational at the same time. Things communicated under the influence of emotions often make the best speeches that will forever be regretted having been given. The end result may be an impasse or a deadlock, and in extreme cases, a ruined relationship. This is definitely not a fertile ground for exploring the options of reaching a sustainable agreement.

In the negotiations I have moderated, I often heard the parties say: "I understand, but…" followed by a counter-proposal. These three words are what I refer to as communication quicksand. Intuitively, most people know that what follows after the *but* is the exact opposite of what the other party just expressed. The phrase "I understand" is only a buffer used to soften the counteroffer. It has little to do with real comprehension; in fact, it may even highlight the exact opposite. Negotiation is not an exercise in oratory skills. In order to master the art of persuasion, executives need to understand what is driving the feelings, thoughts, and actions of the counterpart. Communication starts with listening, and not with talking. The ratio should ideally be 70:30.

Perception is the Only Reality

It is the perception of reality and not reality itself that influences individuals' behavior. People's reactions are based on their subjective perception of reality, consisting of a situation, object, and the other person. The person who is *being perceived* is also acting based on his or her perception of the context (situation, object, and/or person). I will explain this process using the example of my personal experience. During a particularly busy work schedule, I was lecturing in three countries over a period of one week: Poland, France, and Switzerland as the final destination. In Switzerland, I pulled into a gas station to refill the tank and wash my car. Next to the station was a used car dealership. Waiting for the cycle to finish, I wandered over there to take a look at the vehicles on offer. I spotted the salesperson through the window of his office; he briefly looked up but did not pay much attention to me. As I was walking around the lot where the cars were parked, one of them particularly caught my eye. The model, color, production year, extras, and mileage all seemed very attractive. To my surprise, the price was extremely reasonable in relation to the value of the car. Suddenly, very animated, I started inspecting it from all angles. Because I liked the machine so much, in my mind, I started to consider exchanging it for my own car. I excitedly took out my cell phone to consult this rather spontaneous idea with my friend. Just as I was about to dial the number, I saw the salesperson approaching me. Suddenly, his demeanor was much different than when he first saw me through his office window. With a big smile on his face, he was pacing my way with his hand extended to greet me. We exchanged the typical pleasantries. He started his sales talk advertising the car and all it had to offer. Still very much excited, I listened with bright eyes, occasionally nodding my head. I then made my call. He discretely turned away and stood at a distance to allow me some privacy while I talked. I described the situation to my friend, presented the car features, and went on to state the great price. My friend's question was like an accepted ice bucket challenge: "Which currency?" These two words completely changed my perception of what I up to then perceived to be the reality: a very attractive price for a fancy car. In the fervor of the moment and too tired to realize that I have been traveling to countries with different currencies, it slipped my mind that the price for the car was indeed in Swiss francs. No longer so attractive if compared to the Polish currency I had encoded in my head!

When I hung up, the salesman turned back to me with budding hope for securing his commission. The change in dynamics was unmistakable though. Feeling a bit overwhelmed, I thanked him and quickly made my way back to my own car.

Let us now analyze each of the six elements of the perceptual process on the basis of my adventure. The perceptual trigger in this case was an object. While walking around the car dealership arena, I entered the phase of observation, during which I performed a preliminary perceptual selection of one car that caught my eye. Having made a visual assessment of all the other vehicles on display (mark, model, size, color, mileage, extra features, and so on), I then proceeded with the perceptual organization: I compared their prices and contrasted them with the knowledge I had about market prices for similar used cars. Based on this analysis, I made the following interpretation: the vehicle that I liked most was both desirable and affordable for me. My response was to consider exchanging my own car for it and to call and consult my friend about this bold move.

I would like to uncover the dynamics behind the perceptual process and specifically to point out the impact of perception(s) on bargaining power in negotiation. When I first entered the car dealership, my demeanor was completely neutral. I was bored and decided to distract myself by looking at cars while my own one was being washed. The salesperson who spotted me through his office window reacted to me accordingly to his own perception. He saw me as a random visitor and therefore not someone who would merit his attention, energy, and time. If this were a negotiation, my bargaining power would have been on level zero. Due to a perceptual mistake on my part (confusion about currency and exchange rates), I led myself to believe that I spotted a very lucrative deal. In consequence, my whole attitude changed. Enlivened, I walked around and inspected the chosen car with great confidence in my stride. I went from neutral to level one, as would have my bargaining power had this been a negotiation. The shift certainly attracted the attention of the salesperson. He started to perceive me as a potential client and decided to make an effort and leave his desk and approach me with the distant hope of closing a sale. When I completed my scrutiny of the car, I began considering the exchange of cars in my mind. The salesperson perceived this as his *now or never* moment and started giving me his best sales talk to convince me about the deal. My bargaining power would have been at its peak at that stage. The consulting call to my friend caused it to hit rock bottom though.

How does this translate into negotiations? Because of my response to a perceptual trigger, I caused the change in the perceptual process of the salesperson and in turn altered his attitude toward me. In a negotiation, I would have managed to increase my bargaining power, despite an erroneous analysis on my part. Each person can learn how to exercise command over their own perceptual process: the observation, selection, organization, interpretation, and response to a perceptual trigger. This realization can seriously boost the chances of winning a negotiation. By programing the mind into believing something, we can start by improving our mental best alternative to a negotiated agreement (BATNA), which in turn leads to the increase of bargaining power and favorably influences how others perceive and act toward us.

CASE 8

Basic Instincts

IF you follow the evolution of trends in studies on leadership, international business, and people management, you will notice a subtle change taking place. The approach to these topics used to be very technical, with the strategic focus placed on process management and task achievement. Consequently, the methods described would revolve around the application of tools and tactics. Business schools accordingly incorporated this trend in their curricula. It was also reflected in the titles of books on these topics. One will notice the frequency of occurrence of words such as toolkit, handbook, toolbox. The individual seemed not to be a living and feeling entity, and instead was seen as one of the processual elements, and as such, was referred to as capital, a resource, or in milder versions, as talent. From a logical standpoint, it seems a contradiction in terms to approach a person with an objective to *fix* some of the issues they are facing in the same way that you can repair or assemble an item of furniture.

Life always precedes theory. At the dawn of artificial intelligence (AI) replacing a majority of operations, it seems like we taught our executives and business professionals everything they need to know about the mechanic side of human interactions. Modern theory is currently shifting toward a more human-centric approach. Emotional intelligence, secure base leadership, the role of bonding in high-performance leadership, self-empowerment, ego and emotions management are currently topics that are attracting more attention and growing in importance.

A skilled negotiator needs to master the complete package: on the one hand, the strategic side of the process that encompasses all the tools, tactics, and techniques, and on the other, they need to comprehend the personal component for which there is no one-size-for-all tool. Each negotiation is context specific and thus the toolbox might vary, because the human factor is highly volatile and consequently merits a more personalized approach.

The trend switch is also noticeable in real-life business negotiations. The saturation with the strategic component is visible in the way negotiators interact with each other. The skilled ones have received thorough training and have acquired enough experience for their radar to immediately spot the majority of tools and techniques. The effect is that they are cautious and immune to them.

You might have noticed that once the negotiation starts, the parties are on high alert to the moves of the other side. To lower the guards of your negotiation partner, you need to go back to the basics. Forget the elaborate tricks, your counterpart already knows them. Focus instead on the natural instincts, these are the primal reactions that cannot be as easily controlled as the taught ones.

I understood how this works during a negotiation with one of my clients. It was a cold winter day and quite a busy one. I had meetings lined up all morning, and in the afternoon, I was flying to another city for a training session. The negotiation was scheduled to last exactly one hour. All parties were informed about the timeframe and accepted the agenda. If it was prolonged, I would risk missing my flight. My client came with a few people from their support staff, and I was with the colleagues from my team. I was the one who was leading the negotiation; therefore, it was critical that the meeting ends with me still in the room. We could not risk dilution of focus from the main objective or demands being added last minute without me there.

Forty minutes into the meeting, the discussions were still going strong with no end in sight. Five minutes later, I started sending the usual signs, wrapping up the findings, physically organizing the paperwork, then closing the folders in the hope that the parties would pick up on these subtle signs of the meeting coming to an end. They indeed acknowledged that the formal part had come to an end, but it was evident they were not going to leave anytime soon. Staying was not an option for me. I was facing a dilemma. On the one hand, I did not want to rudely cut the meeting short, but on the other, I knew from past experience that this client liked to use the tactic of time pressure to slip in demands right after the meeting had ended, usually in the informal phase. They were deliberately ignoring the nonverbal indicators of closure. Any standard tactics that I would use would be disregarded or countered.

As I looked around the room, trying to stabilize myself, the fur coat of our negotiation partner caught my eye. Without thinking twice, I went to fetch it and stood behind her chair, holding it up for her. As expected, the basic instinct kicked in. She graciously slipped her arms in the sleeves. How long do you think she could stay in a warm meeting room in a heavy fur coat? We ended the meeting in due time, and I managed to catch my flight.

In lack of fur coats and well-heated meeting rooms, you will need to find stimuli that the other party will instinctively react to before they resort to the trained mechanisms. Work on the premise of habitual patterns of behavior related to socially acceptable standards of conduct and business etiquette. Gestures of common courtesy and respect are usually a safe bet.

PART III

Negotiation Booster Implementor

NOW that you have sealed the theoretical foundations with practical examples, you are ready to implement all the acquired skills in your upcoming negotiations. Consequently, the last phase of your *Negotiation Booster* journey is the Implementor. In order to help you systematize all the learnings, this part provides you with the Negotiation Matrix, a legacy for your future negotiations. This matrix is a user-friendly framework, which covers all the steps, phases, and elements of the negotiation process, along with a breakdown indication of what to pay attention to before, during, and after the negotiation. The time you invest in filling it in will reap benefits in the future and save you time during the negotiation.

Your future negotiations will no longer be intuitional; instead, they will begin with a systematic preparation that takes into account all the pieces of the negotiation puzzle that we assembled together. The majority of strategic decisions that you will be making will occur at the time of preparation, when you are most rational due to the limited amount of external emotional stimuli. This is your moment of complete control. If approached properly, it will give your bargaining power an immense boost. When things heat up at the negotiation table, you will benefit from a birds-eye view of the interplay between the various negotiation factors. Use the Negotiation Matrix to monitor your progress and make sure that you are on track toward reaching your desired negotiation outcome at all times.

The Negotiation Matrix

1. Three-level preparation:
   (a) You (self-preparation)
   (b) Internal (your team)
   (c) External (you, your team, and your negotiation partner)
2. Objective—what do you want to achieve?
3. Target—measurable result -> define maximum and minimum
4. Information gathering and profiling of your partner (+ verification of accuracy)
5. Choice of strategy:
   (a) Competition
   (b) Compromise
   (c) Avoidance
   (d) Accommodation
   (e) Collaboration
   (f) Hybrid
6. Team management—distribution of roles within the team
7. Stage setting: room design, virtual space design
8. Agenda design and presentation:
   (a) Welcome to the negotiation
   (b) Items on the agenda
   (c) Common action plan
   (d) Timeframe
9. Opening offer (ZOPA, anchoring)
10. Demands (hierarchy of importance)
11. Identification of interests versus positions
12. BATNA (outside the negotiation)
13. Options (inside the negotiation)
14. Communication (verbal, nonverbal, para-verbal, virtual)
15. The tactics
16. Set milestones and time plan
17. Execution—seal-the-deal

Before the negotiation	During the negotiation	After the negotiation
1		
2		
3		
4	4: Verification of accuracy	
5	5: (Depending on the other party's willingness to cooperate)	
6		
7		
8: Agenda design	8: Agenda presentation to the other party	
	9: Beginning of the negotiation	
10: Demands preparation and order of hierarchy	10: Demands presentation	
	11	
12: Craft alternatives	12: Indicate you have alternatives, do not disclose to the other party	
	13: Explore with the other party	
14: Internal level	14: External level	14: Internal and external
15: Tactics preparation	15: Tactics application	
16	16: Implement time plan	16: Execute time plan
		17

Glossary of Negotiation Terms

Accommodation—referred to as yielding or *lose–win*, an approach that places the relationship first while one's own needs are not satisfied. The level of cooperation is high, but assertiveness is low. A prevalent behavioral pattern exercised in families or between romantic partners.

Anchoring—the limits set forth by the opening offer, which will serve as a reference point around which the other party will structure their offer. Strong signal of expectations and standards.

Anticipatory emotions—the imaginary emotions of how it would feel having already achieved something, used as a motivational tool to boost the chances of obtaining a desired result or spurring to action.

Avoidance—a *lose–lose* negotiation approach synonymous with delay or not taking action. Mediocre both in the level of cooperation between the parties and in the level of individual assertiveness.

BATNA (best alternative to a negotiated agreement)—the fallback position when an agreement in a specific situation or with a particular partner cannot be reached, outside of the negotiation (as opposed to options, which are inside the negotiation).

Boomerang effect—a negative effect of an inadequate opening offer, when the negotiation partner considers the offer as too high and throws back an equally outrageous offer for the sake of reciprocity. The parties risk entering into an ego struggle, which will divert attention from the task.

Chilling effect—a negative effect of an inadequate opening offer, which causes the counterpart to lose interest in the negotiation at the outset. Their perception is that the negotiation is not in good faith.

Cognitive dissonance—a state of the mind in which evidence (objective or fabricated by the other party) conflicts with a person's worldview, values, and beliefs.

Collaboration—a principled approach to negotiation that balances the task and relationship. Synonymous with the popular phrase *win–win*. Centered on finding an agreement that is efficient in the distribution of the resource, is fair to both sides, and reinforces the relationship between them. Involves identifying the interests behind the positions and determining which needs are fixed and which are flexible, and then crafting creative options to bridge those needs.

Competition—one of the negotiation strategies based on power, referred to as the *win–lose* approach. Characterized by forceful behavior, stating demands instead of investigating mutual interests, reluctance to making concessions, and insistence on the satisfaction of one's own needs.

Compromise—the *win–lose* and *lose–win* approach to negotiation because both parties gain and both lose something. An easy and fast means of distribution of a limited resource by splitting it in half, which does not require too much time or creative effort. An approach that does not maximize the benefits of the resource.

Concession—something that one party gives up in exchange for something else in response to a demand of the other party. The conceding party should exchange a good of less value for a good of a higher value.

Counterpart—a noun used to depict the other party at the negotiation table, a label that might lead to a more competitive and aggressive negotiation dynamic.

Deadlock—a situation reached by the negotiation parties, in which each is waiting for the other one to make a move, and they find it difficult to progress. May happen when the parties get stuck in their rigid positions. Requires unblocking or abandoning the negotiation.

Demands—the tokens of trade in a negotiation, which constitute the negotiation mass; should be listed in order of importance and be used for making concessions.

Ego-tiation—the process of negotiation driven by an inordinate need for recognition and approval, dominated by one's ego.

Emotional balcony—a place in your mind that you retreat to in order to gain an objective outlook on the negotiation, where you are the spectator and not the actor, a place where you can manage your emotions and take time for rational decision-making.

Framing—structuring the dynamic to serve one's objective by limiting the options of the other negotiator. Giving a choice within controlled limits, for example, asking the other party which ink they will sign the contract in, blue or black. The choice is theirs, but the only option is signing the contract.

High-context culture—implies that a lot of unspoken information is implicitly transferred during communication. People in a high-context culture tend to place a larger importance on long-term relationships and loyalty and have fewer rules and structure implemented.

Hybrid approach—a mix between the other five negotiation approaches (competition, collaboration, avoidance, accommodation, and compromise), tailored to the type of negotiation partner, the negotiation goal, the negotiation dynamic, and the situational context.

Impasse—a situation when the parties cannot reach an agreement, equivalent to a deadlock.

Implementor—the last step in your self-empowerment journey where you execute the negotiation task. The key focus is the assessment of the implementation of the agenda, strategy, and the objectives you set out to achieve.

Impression management—an attempt to control or alter the impression one makes.

Interests (motives)—the underlying factors behind the position, the reasons why one wants something. See: principal interests.

Low-context culture—implies that a lot of information is exchanged explicitly through the message itself and rarely is anything implicit or hidden. People in low-context cultures tend to have short-term relationships, follow rules and standards closely, and are generally very task-oriented.

Master negotiator—a negotiator who has the mastery of the tools of negotiation and self-empowerment.

Mental map—an inner Global Positioning System (GPS) consisting of life experiences, culture, education, upbringing, and family traditions that influences how an individual perceives the world and that drives their behavior.

Mirror negotiation—the image you display in terms of self-assurance, inner status, and authority that is reflected in the actions of your counterpart and ultimately affects their negotiation approach toward you.

Needs—a continuum of elements that stimulate behavior. According to Maslow's hierarchy of needs, there are five levels of needs: physiological, safety, belonging, esteem, and self-actualization.

Negotiation—a process of perceptual self-management during which two parties with common and opposing needs and interests try to reach a mutually acceptable agreement, which harnesses the needs and interests of both sides. Ideally, a process driven by reason rather than ego or emotions. A negotiation consists of two elements: task and relationship and is driven by scarcity of resources.

Negotiation Booster—a synergetic approach that leverages the task-related aspects of a negotiation with underlying emotional factors. A self-management toolkit designed to tame emotions, ego, and stress by means of personal empowerment.

Negotiation partner—a noun used to depict the other party at the negotiation table, a label that might help shape a more cooperative negotiation dynamic.

Negotiation stack—a collection of negotiation-related skills that work well when combined.

Negotiator—a person with the necessary skillset and training to conduct a negotiation. An individual who sees the big picture (the experts will take care of the details), who can control their emotions, bridge the task and relationship aspects of the negotiation, and execute the negotiation strategy.

Objective—what you want to achieve in a negotiation.

Opening offer—the first offer put on the table in a negotiation, which creates a lasting impression. Should be as close as possible to the other party's barely acceptable terms. See: anchoring

Opponent—a noun used to depict the other party at the negotiation table, a strong label that will lead to a competitive and aggressive negotiation dynamic.

Options—creative solutions introduced when there is no ZOPA, but the parties still want to reach an agreement. Options are inside the negotiation, as opposed to BATNA.

Para-verbal communication—one of the three types of communication (the other two being verbal and nonverbal), depicting how things are expressed: tone, pitch of voice, speed, pace, pauses.

Paradigm shift—the moment when one can see and understand a given situation not only.

Perception errors—an inaccurate way of responding to perceived reality, usually through the lens of one's own mental map, which clouds objective judgment and assessment of the situational context.

Position—the *what do you want* part of the negotiation dynamic. See: interests (motives).

Priming—a form of mental stimulation and thought direction where a stimulus impacts a subsequent stimulus and can lead to the desired behavior. Can be used as a form of persuasion on the subconscious level.

Principal interests—appreciation (sense of recognition or being understood), affiliation (sense of connectedness and belonging), autonomy (freedom to make decisions and take action), status (own standing in comparison to the standing of the other person), role (a job position and associated tasks).

Reciprocity principle—the tendency for people to treat others the way they are treated.

Reinforcement principle—unambiguous, immediate, and clear setting of expectations and standards of conduct that reinforces the desired behavior.

Reservation point—the minimum one is willing to accept before walking away from the negotiation table.

Selective screening—focusing on the most important aspects while blocking all other elements or external triggers that compete for attention.

Shadowing—the presence of a negotiation expert during an important negotiation or for training purposes. The role of the expert is to ensure focus on the execution of the negotiation strategy regardless of the tactics that the other party may use.

Similarity principle—the urge to find a point of similarity that is deeply rooted in human psyche and that brings the negotiation parties closer.

Strategy—a combination of power and cooperation that leads to the negotiation objective.

System of pertinence—as a snapshot of a person's life at a given moment, with all the preoccupations, motivations, dreams, fears, joys, hopes, and so forth linked to the past that shape how the person sees herself or himself, others, and the world.

Tactics—the tools one uses to implement the negotiation strategy. They vary depending on the situational context, the type of negotiation, and the other negotiator.

Tells—a term used in poker when one of the players gives off a signal that unveils how good their cards are. In the negotiation context, tells are signs conveyed by body language that are picked up on by the other party.

Tunnel vision—concentrating only on the problem, failure to see the big picture and creative solutions or alternative courses of action.

Virtual negotiation—an exchange between two parties who are trying to reach an agreement without face-to-face interaction. Can take the form of text-based (instant messaging or e-mail) or voice-based (telephone, videoconference) mode.

Window of Opportunity (WoO)—a favorable opportunity or moment to enter the negotiation, the right place and time to make an opening offer or a demand to a receptive party.

ZOPA (zone of possible agreement)—numerical representation of the overlap between the most that the buyer is willing to pay and the minimum that the seller is willing to accept.

Works Cited

Adams, S. 2019. *Loserthink. How Untrained Brains are Ruining the World.* New York: Portfolio/Penguin.

Adams, S. 2017. *Win Bigly. Persuasion in a World Where Facts Don't Matter.* New York: Portfolio/Penguin.

Annis, B., and J. Gray. 2013. *Work with Me. How Gender Intelligence Can Help You Succeed at Work and in Life.* London: Piatkus.

Barker, A. 2016. *Improve Your Communication Skills.* New York: Kogan Page Limited.

Bergreen, L. 2016. *Casanova. The World of a Seductive Genius.* New York, NY: Simon & Schuster.

Brett, J.M. 2014. *Negotiating Globally. How to Negotiate Deals, Resolve Disputes, and Make Decisions Across Cultural Boundaries.* San Francisco: Jossey-Bass.

Brzezinski, M. 2018. *Know Your Value: Women, Money and Getting What You`re Worth.* Revised Edition. Hachette Books.

Burg, B.M., and J. David. 2018. *The Go-Giver Influencer. A Little Story About a Most Persuasive Idea.* New York, NY: Portfolio/Penguin.

Carnegie, D. 2006. *How to Win Friends and Influence People.* London: Vermilion.

Chu, C.N. 2010. *The Art of War for Women: It`s About the Art, Not the War.* New York, NY: Broadway Books.

Cialdini, R. 2016. *Pre-Suasion. A Revolutionary Way to Influence and Persuade.* London: Random House Books.

Cicero, M.T. 2016. *How to Win an Argument. An Ancient Guide to the Art of Persuasion.* (selected, edited and translated by James M. May). Princeton: Princeton University Press.

Cuddy, A. 2016. *Presence. Bringing Your Boldest Self to Your Biggest Challenges.* London: Orion.

De Beauvoir, S. 2011. *The Second Sex.* London: Vintage.

Dispenza, J. 2014. *You Are the Placebo. Making Your Mind Matter.* London: Hay House UK Ltd.

Duhigg, C. 2014. *The Power of Habit. Why We Do What We Do in Life and in Business.* New York, NY: Random House Trade Paperbacks.

Dutton, K. 2011. *Flipnosis. The Art of Split-Second Persuasion.* London: Arrow Books.

Eger, E. 2017. *The Choice. Even in Hell Hope Can Flower.* London: Rider.

Fleming, K. 2016. *The Leader`s Guide to Emotional Agility. How to Use Soft Skills to Get Hard Results.* Harlow: Pearson Education Limited.

Freud, S. 1922. *Group Psychology and the Analysis of the Ego.* Vienna: The International Psycho-Analytical Press.

Gino, F. 2019. *Rebel Talent. Why it Pays to Break the Rules at Work and in Life.* London: Pan Books.

Greene, R. 2012. *Mastery.* London: Profile Books Ltd.

Greene, R. 1998. *The 48 Laws of Power.* London: Profile Books Ltd.

Greene, R. 2001. *The Art of Seduction.* New York: Penguin Books.

Harkiolakis, N., D. Halkias, S. Abadir. 2016. *e-Negotiations: Networking and Cross-Cultural Business Transactions.* New York, NY: Routledge.

Heinrichs, J. 2017. *Thank You for Arguing. What Cicero, Shakespeare and the Simpsons Can Teach Us About the Art of Persuasion.* London: Penguin Random House UK.

Hill, N. 2005. *Think and Grow Rich.* New York, NY: Jeremy P. Tarcher/Penguin.

Hofstede, G. 2001. *Cultures Consequences: Comparing Values, Behaviors, Institutions, and Organizations Across Nations.* Second Edition. California: Sage Publications.

Holiday, R. 2016. *Ego is the Enemy. The Fight to Master Our Greatest Opponent.* London: Profile Books Ltd.

Jagodzinska, K. 2016. "Egotiation is the New Negotiation: The Concept of Negotiation Revisited". *Eurasian Journal of Business and Management* 4, no. 2, 72–80. doi: 10.15604/ejss.2016.04.02.007 (accessed May 30, 2020.)

Jagodzinska, K. 2016. "How to Manage Perception to Win Negotiations". *International Journal of Social Science Studies* 4, no. 2, 69–77. doi: 10.11114/ijsss.v4i2.1320

Jang, J. 2015. *Rejection Proof. How to Beat Fear and Become Invincible.* London: Random House.

Johnson, S. 1999. *Who Moved My Cheese? An A-mazing Way to Deal with Change in Your Work and in Your Life.* London: Vermilion.

Jung, C.G. 1968. *Man and His Symbols.* USA: Dell Publishing.

Kelly, M. 2016. *Settle for More.* New York, NY: HarperCollins Publishers.

Machiavelli, N. 2011. *The Prince.* UK: Penguin Random House.

Mackay, H. 1997. *Dig Your Well Before You`re Thirsty.* New York, NY: Currency Doubleday.

Mandela, N. 2018. 11 Life Lessons from Nelson Mandela. London: Windmill Books.

Manzoni, J.F., and J.L. Barsoux. 2007. *The Set-Up-To-Fail Syndrome. Overcoming the Undertow of Expectations.* Boston: Harvard Business School Publishing Corporation.

Maslow, A.H. 1954. *Motivation and Personality.* USA: Addison-Wesley Educational Publishers Inc.

Meyer, E. 2015. *The Culture Map: Decoding How People Think, Lead, and Get Things Done Across Cultures*. Philadelphia: Public Affairs.

Mnookin, R.H., S.R. Peppet, A.S. Tulumello. 2000. *Beyond Winning. Negotiating to Create Value in Deals and Disputes*. Cambridge: The Belknap Press of Harvard University Press.

Morgan, N. 2013. "How to Become an Authentic Speaker". HBR's 10 Must Reads on Communication, Boston, Massachusetts: Harvard Business Review Press.

Morrison, T., W.A. Conaway, G.A. Borden. 1994. *Kiss, Bow or Shake Hands*. Avon: Adams Media Corporation.

Obliger, D. 2018. *Life or Death Listening. A Hostage Negotiator's How-to Guide to Mastering the Essential Communication Skill*. USA: Amazon Kindle Direct Publishing.

Obliger, D. 2019. *The 28 Laws of Listening. Best Practices for the Master Listener*. USA: End of the Drive, Secondhand Ranch, Rose Hill.

Sandberg, S, and A. Grant. 2017. *Option B. Facing Adversity, Building Resilience and Finding Joy*. London: WH Allen.

Slocum, J.W., and D. Hellriegel. 2011. *Principles of Organizational Behavior*. South-Western Cengage Learning. – added

Sharrot, T. 2017. *The Influential Mind. What the Brain Reveals About Our Power to Change Others*. London: Abacus.

Tzu, S. 1988. *The Art of War*. Boulder: Shambhala Publications, Inc.

Waal, F.D. 2019. *The Age of Empathy*. London: Souvenir Press.

Ury, W. 1992. *Getting Past No. Negotiating with Difficult People*. London: Century Business.

Williams, G., P. Iyer. 2016. *Body Language Secrets to Win More Negotiations. How to Read Any Opponent and Get What You Want*. Wayne: The Career Press Inc.

References

Babcock, L., and L. Sara. 2008. *Ask for It. How Women Can Use the Power of Negotiation to Get What They Really Want*. New York, NY: Bantam Book.
- An invaluable resource providing women with a guide on how to effectively use negotiation strategies to increase their chances of winning.

Carse, J.P. 2013. *Finite and Infinite Games. A Vision of Life as Play and Possibility*. New York, NY: Free Press.
- A useful guide to understanding the different types of games.

Cohen, H. 1980. *You Can Negotiate Anything*. New York, NY: Lyle Stuart.
- An insightful discussion on how perceived power can get you anything you want in negotiations.

Collins, P. 2009. *Talking Your Way to What You Want. Negotiate to Win!* New York, NY: Sterling Publishing.
- A practical instrument to gaining the upper hand during negotiations.

Dalio, R. 2017. *Principles: Life and Work*. New York, NY: Simon & Schuster.
- A framework of the most effective ways for individuals and companies to make decisions.

Dawson, R. 2011. *Secrets of Power Negotiating. Updated for the 21st Century*. New Jersey, NJ: The Career Press.
- A compilation of new insights on the classic "win-win" strategy.

Dinnar, Samuel, Laurence Susskind. 2019. *Entrepreneurial Negotiation: Understanding and Managing the Relationships that Determine Your Entrepreneurial Success*. New York, NY: Springer.
- This book highlights the skills that entrepreneurs need to acquire to strike better deals.

Dixit, Avinash K, Barry J. Nalebuff. 2010. *The Art of Strategy. A Game Theorist's Guide to Success in Business and Life*. W.W. Norton & Company.
- Useful background reading with significant insight into game theory.

Fisher, R., and U. William. 2012. *Getting to Yes. Negotiating an Agreement Without Giving in*. London: Random House Business Books.
- The great classic on the principled approach to negotiation presenting a straight-forward framework for maximizing gains for both negotiation parties.

Fisher, R., and S. Daniel. 2005. *Beyond Reason. Using Emotions as You Negotiate*. London: Penguin Books.
- A practical guide on how to effectively channel your emotions towards achieving your negotiation goals.

Harvard Business Essentials. 2003. *Negotiation*. Boston: Harvard Business School Publishing.
- A useful tool for preparing for negotiations.

Harvard Business Review. 2011. *Winning Negotiations*. Boston: Harvard Business Review Press.
- An inspiring compilation of perspectives on the success factors of a negotiation.

Hicks, Donna. 2019. *Leading with Dignity: How to Create a Culture that Brings Out the Best in People*. Yale University Press.
- Refreshing insights on how to better understand and apply the concept of dignity in modern leadership.

Karrass, C.L. 1970. *The Negotiating Game. How to Get What You Want*. New York, NY: Thomas Y. Crowell Publishers.
- A persuasive analysis of the power of preparation for a negotiation.

Kennedy, G. 2009. *Negotiation: An A-Z Guide*. London: Profile Books.
- A useful reading showcasing the skills and psychology behind a successful negotiation.

Kolb, D.M., and W. Judith. 2003. *Everyday Negotiation. Navigating the Hidden Agendas in Bargaining*. San Francisco: Jossey-Bass.
- A modern study on interpersonal communication and psychological tactics used in negotiations.

Lewicki, R.J., and M.S. David, and B. Bruce. 2011. *Essentials of Negotiation*. New York, NY: McGraw-Hill.
- A systematic framework of the core negotiation concepts.

Luce, R.D., and R. Howard. 1989. *Games and Decisions*. New York, NY: Dover Publication Inc.
- An excellent non-technical introduction to the world of game theory.

Malhotra, D. 2016. *How to Break Deadlocks and Resolve Ugly Conflicts (Without Money or Muscle). Negotiating the Impossible*. Oakland: Berrett-Koehler Publisher.
- An analysis of the mechanics of successful negotiations.

Moal-Ulvoas, G. 2014. *Business Negotiation*. Louvain-la-Neuve: De Boeck.
- A compilation of managerial experiences regarding negotiation strategies in Europe.

Presman, G. 2016. *Negotiation. How to Craft Agreements that Give Everyone More*. Great Britain: Icon Book.
- A comprehensive discussion on mutually beneficial approaches for successful negotiations.

Reardon, K. 2005. *Becoming a Skilled Negotiator*. New Jersey, NJ: John Wiley & Sons.
- Useful reference for the efficient use of negotiating skills.

Reynolds, N. 2016. *We Have a Deal. How to Negotiate with Intelligence, Flexibility & Power*. Toronto: Icon Books.
- A modern review on how to get what you want in any situation.

Saner, R. 2008. *The Expert Negotiator*. Leiden/Boston: Martinus Nijhoff Publishers.
- An overview of the various forms of scientifically based negotiation skills.

Schranner, M. 2008. *Costly Mistakes: The 7 Biggest Errors in Negotiations*. Germany: Schranner.
- A practical analysis of the most common pitfalls in difficult negotiations.

Schranner, M. 2015. *Negotiations on the Edge: Strategies and Tactical Steps for Difficult Negotiations*. Germany: Schranner.
- A comprehensive toolkit of the strategies and tactics that will allow you to succeed when negotiations get tough.

Sebenius J.K.R., B. Nicholas, and Mnookin, R.H. 2018. *Kissinger the Negotiator: Lessons from Dealmaking at the Highest Level*. New York, NY: Harper Publishing.
- A profound discussion on the political aspects of negotiations.

Shapira, H. 2017. *Gladiators, Pirates and Games of Trust*. London: Watkins Publishing.
- New insights and anecdotes explaining game theory.

Shapiro, D. 2016. *Negotiating the Nonnegotiable. How to Resolve Your Most Emotionally Charged Conflicts*. New York: Penguin.
- A useful reading on how to manage emotions in view of reaching mutually satisfying outcomes.

Stone, D, and P. Bruce, and H. Sheila. 2000. *Difficult Conversations. How to Discuss What Matters Most*. London: Penguin Books.
- An excellent discussion on how to conduct difficult conversations with minimal anxiety and stress.

Thompson, L. 2008. *The Truth About Negotiations*. Dorchester: Pearson Education Limited.
- A compilation of the 53 truths surrounding the art of negotiations.

Ury, W. 1991. *Getting Past No. Negotiating with Difficult People*. Great Britain: Business Books Limited.
- Explores how to counter people who are not open to negotiating.

Ury, W. 2015. *Getting to Yes with Yourself and Other Worthy Opponents*. New York, NY: HarperCollins.
- This book tackles our main adversary in negotiations: ourselves.

Von N.J., and M. Oskar. 2007. *Theory of Games and Economics Behavior*. US: Princeton Classics Editions.
- A classic work on the fundaments of modern game theory.

Voss, C. 2016. *Never Split the Difference. Negotiating as if Your Life Depended on It*. Great Britain: Penguin.

-    A field-tested approach to high-stakes negotiations.

Watkins, M. 2006. *Shaping the Game. The New Leader's Guide to Effective Negotiating*. Boston: Harvard Business School Publishing.

-    A complete framework of negotiation tactics for leaders.

Index

www.ingramcontent.com/pod-product-compliance
Lightning Source LLC
Chambersburg PA
CBHW050500190326
41458CB00005B/1376

* 9 7 8 1 6 3 7 4 2 3 6 5 3 *